marie claire

easy

Thunder Bay Press
An imprint of the Advantage Publishers Group
5880 Oberlin Drive, San Diego, CA 92121-4794
www.thunderbaybooks.com

All notations of errors or omissions should be addressed to Thunder Bay Press, Editorial Department, at the above address. All other correspondence (author inquiries, permissions) concerning the content of this book should be addressed to Murdoch Books Pty Limited, Pier 8/9 23 Hickson Road, Millers Point NSW 2000 Australia.

Author and Stylist: Michele Cranston
Design manager: Vivien Valk
Food preparation: Ross Dobson and Jo Glynn
Editor: Jacqueline Blanchard and Margaret Malone

Photographer: Petrina Tinslay
Concept: Lauren Camilleri
Designer: Jacqueline Richards
Production: Adele Troger

ISBN-13: 978-1-59223-661-9
ISBN-10: 1-59223-661-8
Library of Congress Cataloging-in-Publication Data available upon request.

Printed by 1010 Printing. Printed in China.
1 2 3 4 5 10 09 08 07 06

IMPORTANT: Those who might be at risk from the effects of salmonella poisoning (the elderly pregnant women, young children, and those suffering from immune deficiency diseases) shoul consult their doctor with any concerns about eating raw eggs.

CONVERSION GUIDE: You may find cooking times vary depending on the oven you are using. Fc convection ovens, as a general rule, set the oven temperature to 70°F lower than indicated in th recipe. We have used 4 teaspoon to 1 tablespoon measurements. If you are using 3 teaspoon to 1 tablespoon measure, for most recipes the difference will not be noticeable However, for recipes using baking powder, gelatin, baking soda, or small amounts of flour ar cornstarch, add an extra teaspoon for each tablespoon specified.

marie claire

easy

michele cranston
photography by petrina tinslay

THUNDER BAY
P·R·E·S·S
San Diego, California

contents

Welcome to *Marie Claire Easy*: a selection of our favorite recipes that are simple and light, fruity and sublime, quickly broiled, and lightly tossed with a twist of lemon and lime. This is a hearty book with lots of yummy ideas that we hope will inspire you, with everything from coconut shrimp and chili corn cakes to duck soup and seared snapper, tropical fruit salad, and mango gelatins.

I've had a lot of fun revisiting old favorites, and I hope that you have as much fun cooking and eating from our selection.

michele cranston

ingredient note # papaya and mango

Tropical fruits are one of the great delights of summer. After months of making do with apples, pears, and oranges, there is suddenly an explosion on supermarket shelves of all things sweet, colorful, and exotically perfumed. Think mangoes, melons, lychees, pineapples, and red papayas.

Chilled red papaya is a taste of summer and the tropics. One mouthful can transport you to days of clear skies and endless blue horizons. I love this fruit served simply with a squeeze of lime for breakfast or sliced into a tropical fruit salad. This is a fruit that loves a bit of pepper, so toss it into a bowl with arugula, prosciutto, fresh basil leaves, and a sweet balsamic vinaigrette, or simply add it to a chicken salad.

The first mango of the season is always a taste of good things to come. Richly sweet with a tangy bite, the mango needs only to be chilled and cut to make the perfect finish to a summertime dinner. You can also puree the flesh and serve it with ice cream or fold it through creamy yogurt to have with crisp almond bread. To enhance that summertime taste, finely dice the flesh and add it to a chili salsa for a wonderful accompaniment to broiled fish or chicken.

ingredient note   # lemon

I'm often asked to name ingredients that I can't do without, and my answer is always the same: fresh herbs and lemons. No matter what time of year, you'll always find lemons in my kitchen. To me, they bring a freshness and vitality of flavor to any recipe in which they are used.

Lemon zest contains the oils that perfume the lemon, while the juice contains the flavor. By using a combination of both, you heighten the citrus taste. Imagine seafood without lemon, or a dessert selection without the classic lemon tart. Smoked salmon loves a dollop of lemon mayonnaise, and my favorite crepe comes with just a splash of lemon juice and a sprinkling of sugar. It's also wonderful added to a simple pasta salad of fresh herbs and Parmesan cheese or a bowl of steamed couscous flavored with cilantro and roasted almonds. Lemon also makes a perfect base for chicken and seafood marinades, and there are some vegetables that are lost without its acidic tang, such as asparagus, broccoli, spinach, and zucchini. The grated zest of the lemon brings a citrus bite to cakes and frosting and helps to balance the sweetness of many fruit desserts, so always keep lemons on hand.

winter squash

I know it's an everyday vegetable, but roasted winter squash is one of my all-time favorites. When looking for squash for roasting, I prefer those with a firm flesh that is strongly colored. You don't have to do much to this vegetable to make it taste great. Some oil and seasoning will do the trick, but you can also flavor roasted squash with soy and ginger or add some cumin and garlic to the roasting oil.

Baked squash is ideal for adding to salads that have a bit of a bite. Slightly bitter leaves such as arugula, radicchio, and Belgian endive will be helped with the addition of winter squash and the crunch of some nuts. It goes wonderfully with hazelnuts, sunflower seeds, sesame seeds, pecans, and cashews. When it comes to the winter months, nothing beats a comforting bowl of warmly spiced squash soup. And let's not forget its close relationship to the zucchini and small summer squashes, which provide a dash of color and shape to the vegetable repertoire. Smothered with butter, a squeeze of lemon juice, and a sprinkle of seasoning, they make a wonderful side dish.

ingredient note **orange and mandarin**

Oranges and mandarins have become such common fruits that it is difficult to appreciate just how exotic they once were. Their flavor has taken hold in European cuisines—as a dried peel, orange is evident in most traditional fruitcakes, while the sugared zest is often used to adorn desserts.

Citrus flavors can be used in a variety of ways. They can reduce the richness of meats such as ham, roasted pork, and spiced duck, or they can be enjoyed purely for themselves. A popular combination is a bowl piled high with segments of orange, grapefruit, mandarin, and lime, drizzled with honey and dolloped with creamy yogurt. Just as tasty is a simple side dish of watercress, grated beet, and sliced orange.

Citrus flavors also work well with spices like cinnamon, star anise, cloves, and cardamom. Add orange zest to sweetened mascarpone cheese or enjoy the simple pleasures of an orange or grapefruit sorbet. When a dessert calls for the use of orange, it is often nice to add a bit of a twist by using mandarin instead. The mandarin has a slightly more perfumed flavor and will surprise and delight the taste buds.

walnut and soda bread stuffed mushrooms squash muffins
with marmalade corn bread walnut corn bread with bacon
honeyed nuts scrambled egg tartlets potato latkes with
smoked salmon coconut shrimp ceviche with coconut dressing
duck and marmalade turnovers salmon in pastry pickled
salmon potato pizza shrimp toasts citrus scallop wontons
seared salmon on brioche with saffron mayonnaise squid
stuffed with lemon risotto shrimp balls steamed

01   starters and sides

shrimp wontons ma hor on pineapple pistachio and orange
crackers goat cheese tartlets chicken and mushroom wontons
chili corn cakes sweet pork wontons corn and shrimp
pancakes whiting and squash tempura artichoke tartlets
fish cakes shrimp sandwich tiny brioche with garlic shrimp

walnut and soda bread

makes 1 loaf

3²/3 cups all-purpose flour
1 heaping teaspoon baking soda
1 heaping teaspoon cream of tartar
1 tablespoon sugar
1 teaspoon sea salt
2 cups buttermilk
4 tablespoons finely chopped walnuts
3 tablespoons butter, plus extra,
   softened, to serve

Preheat the oven to 400°F. Put the all-purpose flour, baking soda, cream of tartar, sugar, and sea salt into a large bowl. Make a well in the center and gradually add the buttermilk, combining to form a soft dough. Add the walnuts and slowly fold through the dough.

Melt the 3 tablespoons butter and brush the insides of a 4 x 8¹/4-inch loaf pan with it. Put the dough into the greased pan and pour any remaining butter over it.

Bake for 30 minutes, then reduce the oven temperature to 300°F and bake for an additional 30 minutes, or until a skewer inserted into the center comes out clean. Turn the bread out onto a wire rack to cool. Serve warm or toasted with butter, apricot jam, honey, or ricotta cheese.

stuffed mushrooms makes 18

1/4 cup ricotta cheese
1/2 teaspoon finely chopped marjoram
1/4 teaspoon finely chopped rosemary
2 slices prosciutto, finely sliced
2 teaspoons virgin olive oil
salt and freshly ground black pepper,
  to season
18 button mushrooms

Preheat the oven to 350°F. In a bowl, combine the ricotta, herbs, prosciutto, and oil. Season well with salt and freshly ground black pepper. Remove the stems from the mushrooms and trim their rounded tops with a sharp knife to give them a flat base when laid upside down on the work surface. Spoon the ricotta filling into the center of the mushrooms and put them on a baking sheet. Season with salt and pepper and bake for 12–15 minutes.

squash muffins
with marmalade

makes 36

2 cups peeled and chopped winter
  squash
1 1/4 cups self-rising flour
1/2 teaspoon grated nutmeg
pinch salt
1/2 cup superfine sugar
1 large egg
2 tablespoons plain yogurt
2 1/2 tablespoons butter, melted, plus
  extra, softened, to serve
1/3 cup pine nuts, toasted
bitter orange marmalade, to serve

Put the squash in a saucepan of water and boil until tender. Drain and mash the squash.

Preheat the oven to 350°F. Sift the flour, nutmeg, and salt into a large bowl, stir in the sugar, and make a well in the center of the dry ingredients. In a separate bowl, beat together the egg, yogurt, mashed squash, and melted butter. Pour into the well of the flour mixture. Stir until just combined.

Gently stir the pine nuts through the dough and spoon into three 12-hole, greased mini muffin pans (lined with paper muffin cups if desired). Bake for 10–12 minutes, then cool on a wire rack. Slice in half and serve with butter and bitter orange marmalade.

corn bread

$1/2$ cup milk
$1/2$ cup butter
2 cups all-purpose flour
2 teaspoons baking powder
2 teaspoons baking soda
$12/3$ cups fine cornmeal
1 teaspoon sea salt
2 eggs
$1/2$ cup buttermilk
1 handful cilantro leaves, roughly
  chopped
2 red chilies, seeded and finely
  chopped

Preheat the oven to 350°F. Put the milk into a saucepan with the butter. Heat over low heat until the butter has melted, then remove from the heat.

Sift the flour, baking powder, and baking soda into a bowl. Add the fine cornmeal and sea salt and make a well in the center.

In a separate bowl, whisk together the eggs, buttermilk, cilantro, and chilies. Fold the egg mixture through the dry ingredients, then fold through the warm milk mixture. Pour the batter into a greased $91/2$-inch springform cake pan and mark the top into wedges. Bake for 25 minutes, or until the corn bread is golden brown and a skewer inserted into the center comes out clean. Serve warm with crispy bacon and roasted tomatoes.

walnut corn bread with bacon

makes 48

1 tablespoon walnut oil
1 cup milk
1/2 cup unsalted butter
5 slices bacon, finely sliced
12/3 cups cornmeal
21/2 cups all-purpose flour
2 teaspoons baking powder
1 teaspoon baking soda
1/2 teaspoon salt
3 eggs
1/3 cup plain yogurt
3 scallions, finely sliced
2/3 cup coarsely chopped walnuts
salted butter, to serve

Preheat the oven to 350°F. Lightly grease two 12-hole mini muffin pans with walnut oil (lined with paper muffin cups if desired). Warm the milk and butter in a saucepan. When the butter has melted, remove from the heat.

Put the bacon in a frying pan and cook until it has browned but is not crisp. Remove from the heat.

Meanwhile, sift the dry ingredients into a mixing bowl and make a well in the center. Whisk the eggs with the yogurt and warm milk and fold into the dry ingredients until just blended. Add the scallions, walnuts, and bacon and lightly fold them through the batter.

Spoon half the mixture into the prepared mini muffin pans and bake for 15–20 minutes, or until golden. Repeat with the remaining mixture. Serve warm, spread with butter.

honeyed nuts

2 tablespoons honey
1 teaspoon butter
1/2 cup almonds
1/2 cup pine nuts
1/2 cup sunflower seeds
1/2 cup sesame seeds
squeeze of lemon juice
plain yogurt, to serve

In a small saucepan, warm the honey and butter. Add the nuts and seeds, and stir over low heat until well coated. Remove from the heat and squeeze a little lemon juice over the nuts. Serve with yogurt.

scrambled egg tartlets

makes 24

2 slices prosciutto, each sliced into
  12 pieces
4 eggs
3/4 cup whipping cream
salt and freshly ground black pepper,
  to season
2 tablespoons butter
24 prebaked short-crust tartlet shells
  (see basics)

Preheat the oven to 350°F. Put the slices of prosciutto on a baking sheet lined with waxed paper and broil or bake until crisp. Remove and drain on paper towels.

Put the eggs and cream in a bowl and lightly whisk together. Season well with salt and freshly ground black pepper. Put half the butter in a nonstick frying pan over medium heat and add half the egg mixture. Slowly fold together. When just set, remove from the heat. Spoon the cooked mixture into half of the prebaked tartlet shells and top each one with a piece of prosciutto. Grease the frying pan with the rest of the butter and repeat the process with the remaining mixture. Serve immediately.

potato latkes with smoked salmon

makes 45

3 tablespoons butter
2 leeks, white part only, finely chopped
2 tablespoons thyme leaves
2 1/2 cups peeled and grated potato
2 eggs, lightly beaten
1/3 cup all-purpose flour
salt and freshly ground black pepper,
  to season
vegetable oil, for cooking
5 1/2 ounces smoked salmon

Heat the butter in a small saucepan. Add the leeks and thyme, and cook over low heat for 15–20 minutes, stirring occasionally, until the leeks are soft and slightly caramelized. Set aside to cool.

Mix together the grated potato, eggs, and flour and season well with salt and freshly ground black pepper. Put the mixture into a sieve set over a bowl and press down to remove any excess moisture.

Add enough vegetable oil to a frying pan to come to a depth of 1/4 inch. Heat the oil over medium heat and add heaping teaspoons of the potato mixture. Flatten a little and cook each side for 4–5 minutes, or until golden, then remove and drain well on paper towels. Repeat until all the mixture has been cooked.

To assemble, cut the salmon into forty-five 1/4-inch lengths. Put a slice of salmon on each latke and top with a small amount of leek.

coconut shrimp

makes 20

4 egg whites
1 cup all-purpose flour
1 cup dried coconut
2/3 cup oil
20 raw shrimp, peeled and deveined
  with tails intact
sweet chili and ginger sauce, to serve
lime wedges, to serve

Whisk the egg whites until they are light and fluffy. Put the flour and coconut onto two separate plates. Heat a deep pan or wok and add the oil. While the oil is heating, toss the first shrimp in the flour, dip it into the egg white, and then roll it in the coconut. Set aside. Repeat the process with the remaining shrimp.

Once the oil has reached the frying point (if you drop a coconut shred into the oil it will sizzle), carefully lower the shrimp into the oil in batches of five. When the coconut has turned light brown on one side, turn the shrimp over and cook until they are crisp and golden on both sides. Remove the shrimp and drain on paper towels.

Serve with a sweet chili and ginger sauce and a squeeze of fresh lime.

ceviche with coconut dressing

makes 40

18 ounces firm white-fleshed fish, skin removed and boned
3 limes, juiced
scant 1/2 cup coconut milk
1 teaspoon grated fresh ginger
1/2 teaspoon ground turmeric
1 teaspoon sugar
1 tablespoon finely chopped cilantro root
1/2 teaspoon salt
2 scallions, finely sliced on the diagonal

Slice the fish into bite-sized pieces and put in a glass or ceramic dish. Cover with the lime juice and refrigerate for 2 hours. Put the coconut milk, ginger, turmeric, sugar, cilantro root, and salt in a bowl and stir to combine. Drain the fish and add to the coconut dressing. Sprinkle with the scallion and serve.

duck and marmalade turnovers

1 1/2 tablespoons butter

1 cup finely chopped onions

1 garlic clove, crushed

1/3 cup finely diced pancetta

1 teaspoon thyme leaves

1/2 cup red wine

1 large boneless duck breast, finely diced

2 tablespoons bitter orange marmalade

1/4 cup ground almonds

salt and freshly ground black pepper, to season

30 short-crust pastry rounds, 3 inches in diameter (see basics)

1 egg, beaten

Heat the butter in a small frying pan over medium heat. Add the onion and garlic and cook for 5–7 minutes, or until the onion is transparent. Add the pancetta and thyme and cook for an additional 5 minutes before adding the wine and diced duck breast. Reduce the heat to low and simmer, covered, for 20 minutes, or until the liquid has been absorbed. Remove the cover and return the heat to medium. Add the marmalade and ground almonds and stir and cook for 2 minutes, or until the mixture has thickened. Remove from the heat and season with salt and freshly ground black pepper. Set aside to cool.

Preheat the oven to 350°F. Brush the edges of the pastry rounds with the beaten egg. Put a heaping teaspoon of the filling in the center of each pastry round and fold in half. Seal the edges with a fork and put the turnovers on a baking sheet lined with waxed paper. Brush with more beaten egg and bake for 20 minutes, or until golden brown.

salmon in pastry   makes 30

10½ ounces whole salmon fillet, boned
   and skin removed
2 teaspoons sumac
1 teaspoon grated fresh ginger
½ cup unsalted butter, cut into cubes
   and softened
1 tablespoon candied ginger, finely
   chopped
1 tablespoon currants
1 Kaffir lime leaf, finely sliced
2 sheets ready-made puff pastry,
   thawed
2 tablespoons milk

Preheat the oven to 400°F. Cut the salmon lengthwise into four ¾-inch-wide strips. Put the sumac, ginger, softened butter, candied ginger, currants, and Kaffir lime leaf in a bowl and mix until soft and well combined.

Slice the pastry sheets in half and lie a piece of salmon along the center of each one. Top each with a quarter of the flavored butter and fold the pastry around the salmon, pressing the edges together at the top to form a seal. Put the salmon wraps on a baking sheet lined with waxed paper, ensure that the pastry is well sealed, and brush with a little milk. Bake for 20–25 minutes, or until golden brown. Remove and allow to cool until just warm. Slice into 1-inch-wide portions and serve.

pickled salmon

makes 30

2 tablespoons sweet Japanese pickled
  ginger juice
2 teaspoons pickled ginger, finely
  sliced
1 tablespoon grated fresh ginger
1 teaspoon light soy sauce
1 teaspoon fish sauce
2 tablespoons lime juice
33/4 ounces whole salmon fillet, boned
  and skin removed
1 tablespoon finely chopped mint
  leaves
30 Belgian endive leaves, washed and
  drained
2 teaspoons toasted sesame seeds

In a small bowl, combine the ginger juice, pickled ginger, fresh ginger, soy sauce, fish sauce, and lime juice.

Slice the salmon in half lengthwise and then slice each half thinly. Put the salmon in the ginger dressing and allow it to marinate for 5–10 minutes. Add the mint and toss to combine. Put a tablespoon of the mixture into each of the Belgian endive leaves. Sprinkle with the toasted sesame seeds and serve immediately.

potato pizza

serves 4

4 medium all-purpose potatoes, peeled
  and finely sliced
2 ready-made medium pizza bases
  (see basics)
extra-virgin olive oil
1 tablespoon finely chopped rosemary
sea salt, to sprinkle

Preheat the oven to 400°F. Arrange the potato slices on the pizza bases. Drizzle liberally with extra-virgin olive oil and sprinkle with the rosemary. Sprinkle with some sea salt and bake for 20 minutes. Remove from the oven and drizzle with a little olive oil. This simple pizza is wonderful partnered with hearty winter soups or served as an appetizer.

shrimp toasts

1¹/2 cups raw shrimp meat
1 garlic clove, crushed
2 tablespoons chopped scallions
1 teaspoon grated fresh ginger
1 teaspoon sugar
1 teaspoon sesame oil
1 tablespoon cornstarch
2 teaspoons finely chopped cilantro
  leaves
1 teaspoon grated lemon zest
1 teaspoon salt
8 slices white bread, crusts removed
2 tablespoons sesame seeds
peanut oil, for frying

Put the shrimp meat, garlic, scallions, ginger, sugar, sesame oil, cornstarch, cilantro, lemon zest, and salt in a food processor and process in short bursts until the mixture is smooth and well mixed.

Cut each slice of bread into quarters, spread the shrimp mixture thickly on each piece of bread, and sprinkle with the sesame seeds.

Put the peanut oil in a frying pan to a depth of ¹/2 inch. Heat the oil over moderate heat and cook the bread, shrimp-side down, until golden. Turn and quickly cook the other side. Serve hot.

citrus scallop wontons

makes 30

1¹/₄ cups white scallop meat
¹/₂ teaspoon grated orange zest
3 tablespoons finely chopped
   cilantro leaves
3 tablespoons finely sliced scallions
¹/₄ teaspoon sesame oil
1 large red chili, seeded and
   finely chopped
1 teaspoon fish sauce
1 Kaffir lime leaf, finely sliced
¹/₄ teaspoon finely grated fresh ginger
2 tablespoons all-purpose flour
30 square wonton wrappers
peanut oil, for deep-frying
lime wedges, to serve

Dice the scallop meat and put it into a bowl with the orange zest, cilantro, scallions, sesame oil, chili, fish sauce, Kaffir lime leaf, and ginger. Stir to combine, then sprinkle with the all-purpose flour and stir again.

Put 1 wonton wrapper on a clean work surface and moisten the edges with a little water. Place 1 teaspoon of the filling in the center, then bring the four corners together, sealing the sides. Repeat with the remaining mixture. Put the wontons on a baking sheet lined with waxed paper. To cook, deep-fry in the peanut oil and serve with fresh lime wedges.

seared salmon on brioche with saffron mayonnaise

makes 20

five 3/4-inch-thick slices of brioche loaf,
  crusts removed
20 saffron threads
2 egg yolks
2 teaspoons lemon juice
salt and freshly ground black pepper,
  to season
3/4 cup vegetable oil
7-ounce salmon fillet
2 teaspoons olive oil, for frying
20 sprigs chervil, to serve

Cut each slice of brioche into four squares. Put the saffron in a small saucepan with 1/4 cup of water. Put over medium heat and reduce until only a tablespoon of liquid remains. Remove from the heat and allow to cool. Put the egg yolks and lemon juice in a blender and season with salt and pepper. Blend, and with the motor still running, slowly drizzle in the vegetable oil until a thick mayonnaise forms. Pour into a bowl and fold through the saffron water and threads. Set aside.

Season the salmon with salt and freshly ground black pepper. Heat the olive oil in a frying pan over high heat and sear the salmon on both sides, turning once. Reduce the heat and cook for an additional 5 minutes. Cool and break the fish up into flakes.

Lightly toast the brioche squares. Top with a little of the mayonnaise, some salmon, and a sprig of chervil.

calamari stuffed with lemon risotto

makes 24 slices

3 cups fish or vegetable stock
(see basics)
2 tablespoons butter
1 cup finely diced onion
1 garlic clove, crushed
1 teaspoon thyme leaves
1 cup arborio (risotto) rice
1 tablespoon finely chopped
lemon zest
2 tablespoons lemon juice
1/2 cup roughly chopped Italian
parsley
salt and freshly ground black pepper,
to taste
6 medium squid, each approximately
6 inches long

Preheat the oven to 350°F. Heat the stock in a saucepan and keep at a low simmer. Melt the butter in a separate pan over medium heat and cook the onion, garlic, and thyme leaves, stirring occasionally, for 5–7 minutes, or until the onion is transparent. Add the rice and zest and stir well until coated. Add 1/2 cup of the hot stock and stir constantly over medium heat until all the liquid has been absorbed. Continue adding more liquid, 1/2 cup at a time, until all the liquid has been absorbed and the rice is creamy and tender. Remove the pan from the heat and add the lemon juice, parsley, salt, and freshly ground black pepper.

Clean the squid, removing the tentacles from the body. Stuff the body with the risotto and put in a roasting pan with 1/2 cup of water or stock. Cover with aluminum foil and bake for 30 minutes. Remove and allow to cool a little before slicing at 3/4-inch intervals.

shrimp balls

1/4 cup rice flour
1/4 teaspoon salt
24 large raw shrimp, shelled and
   deveined
2 1/2 teaspoons mirin
1 egg white, lightly beaten
1/3 cup finely sliced scallions
salt and freshly ground black pepper,
   to season
3 1/2 ounces somen noodles, broken
   into small pieces
1/2 cup peanut oil

dipping sauce
2 tablespoons lime juice
2 tablespoons mirin
4 tablespoons soy sauce

Sift the flour and salt into a bowl. Make a well in the center and gradually add 2 tablespoons of water, whisking to make a smooth paste. Set aside.

Grind or finely chop the shrimp meat. Put in a bowl and stir in the mirin, egg white, scallions, and the flour paste. Season with salt and freshly ground black pepper and mix well to combine.

Spread the broken noodles on a sheet of waxed paper. Roll 1/2-tablespoon amounts of the shrimp mixture into balls and then roll them in the broken noodles. Set aside.

To make the sauce, combine the lime juice, mirin, and soy sauce.

Heat the oil in a wok or deep frying pan over medium heat and cook the shrimp balls until golden, turning if necessary. Drain on paper towels and serve with the dipping sauce.

steamed shrimp wontons

makes 24

2 egg whites
1 cup ground shrimp meat
1/2 teaspoon sea salt
1/4 teaspoon Chinese five-spice
1/2 cup finely sliced scallions
1 teaspoon finely grated fresh ginger
24 square wonton wrappers
lemon dipping sauce (see basics), to
  serve

Lightly whisk the egg whites in a large bowl. Add the ground shrimp meat, sea salt, five-spice powder, scallions, and ginger. Stir to combine.

Put 1 square wonton wrapper onto a clean work surface and moisten the edges with a little water. Put a heaping teaspoon of the filling mixture into the center of the wrapper and then bring the four corners together, sealing the edges. Set aside and repeat with the remaining mixture.

Put the wontons into a bamboo steamer basket lined with oiled waxed paper. Set the basket over a large saucepan of boiling water and steam for 10–12 minutes. Serve with the lemon dipping sauce.

ma hor on pineapple   makes 20

2 garlic cloves, roughly chopped
2 tablespoons roughly chopped
   cilantro root
1/2 teaspoon green peppercorns
1 teaspoon grated fresh ginger
2 scallions, chopped
2 tablespoons peanut oil
2/3 cup ground pork
1/4 cup ground shrimp meat
1/2 teaspoon finely chopped Kaffir
   lime leaves
11/2 tablespoons jaggery (or brown
   sugar)
11/2 tablespoons fish sauce
1 pineapple, quartered, core removed
2 chilies, seeded and finely sliced,
   to garnish

Put the garlic, cilantro root, pepper-corns, ginger, scallions, and oil in a blender and pulse until smooth. Heat a frying pan over medium heat, add the paste, and cook for 2 minutes. Add the pork and shrimp meat and continue to cook, stirring occasionally, until the meat has colored. Add the Kaffir lime leaves, sugar, and fish sauce, reduce the heat, and cook until the mixture is slightly sticky. Allow to cool. Slice the quartered pineapple into 1/2-inch-thick triangles, top with the cooled mixture, and garnish with the chilies.

pistachio and orange crackers

makes 30

1 cup all-purpose flour
1/4 cup rice flour
1/4 teaspoon baking powder
scant 1 1/2 teaspoons salt
2 teaspoons chopped orange zest
1/4 cup chopped pistachios
freshly ground black pepper, to season
3 tablespoons vegetable oil
1/3 cup plain yogurt
1 egg white, lightly whisked
sea salt, to season

Preheat the oven to 350°F. Sift the flours, baking powder, and salt into a bowl. Add the orange zest, pistachios, and some freshly ground black pepper and mix well. Add the oil and yogurt and mix to form a dough. Lightly knead until smooth, then put on a floured work surface and roll out as thinly as possible. Cut out crackers with a 1 1/2-inch round cookie cutter or into 1 1/2-inch squares, brush with the egg white and season with sea salt. Put onto baking sheets lined with waxed paper and cook in batches in the oven for 15 minutes or until golden brown. Cool on wire racks. Serve with a sharp cheddar cheese or with crème fraîche and smoked trout.

goat cheese tartlets

makes 36

1 cup goat cheese
1 cup whipping cream
1 egg, beaten
3 egg yolks
salt and freshly ground black pepper,
  to season

phyllo pastry tartlet shells
2 ready-made phyllo pastry sheets
3 1/2 tablespoons butter, melted
thyme leaves, finely chopped

Preheat the oven to 315°F. Put the two phyllo pastry sheets onto a clean, dry cutting board. Cut in half lengthwise and put one half on top of the other. Cut in half lengthwise again and repeat the process until you have a pile of pastry squares about 2 x 2 3/4 inches in size.

Lightly butter three 12-hole shallow muffin pans or tartlet pans. Line each of the molds with one sheet of phyllo, pressing the pastry well into the sides. Brush with melted butter and scatter some thyme leaves on top. Cover with a second piece of phyllo pastry, brush with butter, and bake for a few minutes until the pastry is lightly golden. Remove and allow to cool.

Increase the oven to 350°F. Crumble the goat cheese into a bowl. Slowly add the cream, mashing until the mixture is smooth and creamy. Fold in the egg and egg yolks and season well with salt and freshly ground black pepper. Pour the mixture into the tart shells and bake for 12 minutes, or until puffed and golden.

chicken and mushroom wontons

4 dried shiitake mushrooms
1 cup ground chicken
4 tablespoons finely chopped bamboo
  shoots
2 tablespoons light soy sauce
1 teaspoon finely grated fresh ginger
1/2 teaspoon sesame oil
24 square wonton wrappers
plum sauce (see basics), to serve

Soak the shiitake mushrooms in hot water for 30 minutes. Drain the mushrooms, squeeze out any excess moisture, and cut off the tough stalks. Finely chop the mushrooms and put them into a bowl with the chicken, bamboo shoots, soy sauce, ginger, and sesame oil. Gently stir to combine the filling ingredients.

Put a wonton wrapper on a clean work surface and moisten the edge with water. Put a heaping teaspoon of the filling into the center and draw all the edges together. Pinch the edges together to form little bags. Put on a baking sheet lined with waxed paper and repeat with the remaining mixture. Steam for 15 minutes in a bamboo steamer and serve with plum sauce.

chili corn cakes   makes 24

2 corncobs
3/4 cup all-purpose flour
1 teaspoon baking powder
1 egg
1 1/2 tablespoons melted butter
1/2 teaspoon salt
3 tablespoons milk
1 teaspoon Tabasco sauce
vegetable oil

Remove the kernels from the corncobs. Put the flour, baking powder, egg, melted butter, and salt into a mixing bowl. Stir to combine. Add the milk and Tabasco sauce to form a thick batter, then add the corn and stir through. Heat some vegetable oil in a deep, heavy-based frying pan over medium heat. Test if the oil is sizzling hot by dropping in a little batter. Then drop small spoonfuls of the batter into the oil and fry on each side until golden brown. Remove and drain on paper towels. Serve while still warm.

sweet pork wontons

makes 24

1¹/4 cups ground pork
¹/2 teaspoon sea salt
1 teaspoon light soy sauce
1 tablespoon Chinese rice wine
3 scallions, finely sliced
¹/2 teaspoon Chinese five-spice
1 teaspoon finely grated fresh ginger
24 square wonton wrappers
peanut oil, for deep-frying
Chinese black vinegar, to serve

Put the pork, sea salt, light soy sauce, rice wine, scallions, five-spice powder, and fresh ginger in a bowl. Stir to combine.

Put a square wonton wrapper on a clean work surface and moisten the edges with a little water. Put a heaping teaspoon of the filling mixture in the center of the wrapper and then fold the wrapper in half to form a triangle. Press to seal the edges, then bring the two pointy ends together over the top of the filling to form a bundle. Put the wontons on a baking sheet lined with waxed paper and repeat with the remaining mixture. To cook, deep-fry in peanut oil and serve with a small dipping bowl of Chinese black vinegar.

corn and shrimp pancakes

makes 40 small pancakes

1/2 cup raw shrimp meat
2 cups corn kernels
2 large eggs
3 tablespoons cornstarch
1/3 cup Asian dried shrimp
1 cup chopped cilantro leaves
2 garlic cloves, finely chopped
2 tablespoons green peppercorns
1 tablespoon sugar
1 tablespoon Worcestershire sauce
1/2 cup peanut oil, for frying

Put the shrimp meat and half of the corn kernels in a food processor and process to a coarse paste. Scrape the paste into a separate bowl and add the rest of the ingredients, except for the oil. Mix well. Heat the oil in a frying pan over medium heat and cook tablespoons of the mixture in batches, turning the pancakes once until crisp and golden. Serve warm.

whiting and squash tempura

makes 40 pieces

1/4 small winter squash, peeled
10 large whiting or firm whitefish
  fillets, bones removed
1 1/4 cups tempura flour
2 cups canola oil, for deep-frying
cilantro leaves, to garnish

dipping sauce
2 tablespoons lemon juice
1/3 cup soy sauce
2 tablespoons mirin
2 teaspoons pickled ginger juice

Slice the squash into 1/8-inch-thick slices and set aside. Slice the whiting fillets in half lengthwise.

To make the dipping sauce, combine the lemon juice, soy sauce, mirin, and pickled ginger juice in a small bowl. Set aside.

Put the tempura flour in a bowl, add 1 cup of iced water, and stir gently with chopsticks until the mixture is just combined and slightly lumpy.

Heat the oil in a wok or deep frying pan over medium heat. Dip the squash slices in the batter and cook in batches for 2–3 minutes, or until lightly golden. Dip the whiting in the batter and cook in batches until lightly golden. Dip the cilantro leaves in the batter and cook for a few seconds. Drain all the tempura and serve hot, accompanied by the dipping sauce.

artichoke tartlets   makes 20

2/3 cup bottled artichoke hearts in oil,
   drained
15 garlic cloves, roasted until soft
1/4 cup olive oil
1/2 teaspoon truffle oil
salt and freshly ground black pepper,
   to season
20 prebaked short-crust tartlet shells
   (see basics)
1/4 cup shaved Parmesan cheese

Put the artichoke hearts, roasted garlic, olive oil, and truffle oil in a blender or food processor and blend until smooth. Season according to taste with salt and freshly ground black pepper. Put 1 teaspoon of the mixture into each of the tartlet shells and top with the shaved Parmesan.

fish cakes

makes 24

4 Kaffir lime leaves, 2 very finely sliced
18-ounce salmon fillet
2 cups fresh bread crumbs
2 eggs
1/2 cup sliced scallions
2 tablespoons finely chopped
   lemongrass
2 tablespoons finely chopped
   cilantro leaves
2 large red chilies, seeded and finely
   chopped
1 tablespoon lime juice
1 teaspoon fish sauce
1/2 teaspoon white pepper
vegetable oil, for frying
lemon wedges, to serve

Put 1 cup of water and 2 whole Kaffir lime leaves in a frying pan over high heat. Bring to a boil, then add the salmon fillet and cover. Reduce the heat and simmer for 5 minutes. Remove from the heat.

Using a fork, break up the cooled salmon and put in a large bowl with the fresh bread crumbs, eggs, finely sliced Kaffir lime leaves, scallions, lemongrass, cilantro, chilies, lime juice, fish sauce, and white pepper. Stir to combine and then shape into 24 small patties.

Heat some vegetable oil in a nonstick frying pan over medium heat. Cook the fish cakes, in batches, until golden. Serve with lemon wedges.

shrimp sandwich

lime mayonnaise

2 egg yolks
1 lime, zested and juiced
1 cup light olive oil
sea salt, to season

20 raw shrimp, peeled and deveined
1/4 cup lime juice
1/4 cup light olive oil
2 tablespoons vegetable oil, for frying
8 slices white sourdough bread
cilantro leaves, to serve
white pepper, to season

To make the lime mayonnaise, whisk the egg yolks and lime zest and juice in a large bowl. Slowly drizzle in the oil while whisking until the mixture thickens, and keep whisking the mixture until it becomes thick and creamy. Season to taste with sea salt. If the mixture is very thick, add a little cold water until you achieve the right consistency.

Put the shrimp, lime juice, and light olive oil into a bowl and leave to marinate for half an hour.

Heat some of the vegetable oil in a heavy-based frying pan over high heat. Put a few of the shrimp into the pan and sear for about 2 minutes, until they begin to curl. Flip them over and continue to cook for an additional minute, or until they are cooked through. Cook the rest of the shrimp, a few at a time, in the same way until all are done.

Spread some lime mayonnaise onto each slice of bread. Divide the shrimp between four slices, sprinkle with cilantro leaves, and season with a little white pepper. Top with the remaining bread slices.

tiny brioche with garlic shrimp

makes 36

1 quantity of brioche dough (see basics), at room temperature
1 egg yolk
1 tablespoon milk
6$^{1}/_{2}$ tablespoons butter
3 garlic cloves, crushed
14 ounces small raw shrimp, peeled
salt and pepper, to season
3 tablespoons lemon juice
1 tablespoon finely chopped Italian parsley

Grease three 12-hole mini muffin pans. Break off walnut-sized balls of brioche dough and put them into the holes. Cover with plastic wrap or a dish towel and allow them to rise in a warm place for 3 hours. Preheat the oven to 350°F. Make an egg wash by whisking the egg yolk with the milk in a bowl.

When the dough has doubled in size, glaze the brioche with the egg wash, then bake for 20–30 minutes, or until golden brown. Remove from the oven and allow to cool.

Put the butter and garlic in a large, heavy-based frying pan and cook over medium heat for 2–3 minutes. Add the shrimp and season. Cook for 3 minutes, turning once, then add the lemon juice and parsley. Remove the shrimp from the pan, reserving the butter sauce. With a sharp knife, remove the tops of the brioches and scoop out about a teaspoonful of bread from the center of each to make a deep hole. Fill with the warm shrimp and spoon over a little of the butter sauce before replacing the brioche lid.

shrimp and water chestnut wontons with plum sauce

serves 36

1 pound raw shrimp, chopped, or
  1 cup shrimp meat
1/2 cup finely diced water chestnuts
1/2 cup finely sliced scallions
2 tablespoons mirin
1/2 teaspoon sesame oil
2 teaspoons fish sauce
1 teaspoon sea salt
ground black pepper, to season
1 egg
36 round wonton wrappers
peanut oil, for deep-frying
plum sauce (see basics), to serve

Put the shrimp meat, water chestnuts, scallions, mirin, sesame oil, fish sauce, sea salt, and some ground black pepper in a bowl and stir to combine. Beat the egg in a small bowl with 1/4 cup of water. Put one of the wonton wrappers on a clean work surface and put a teaspoon of the shrimp mixture in the center. Brush a little of the egg wash around the edges and bring together, sealing the sides, and twist the top firmly.

Transfer to a baking sheet lined with waxed paper and repeat the process with the remaining mixture.

Heat the oil in a wok or deep frying pan and fry the wontons until they are golden brown. Remove and serve with the plum sauce.

fig roll with pecorino

makes 40 slices

1 1/3 cups finely chopped dried figs
2 1/2 teaspoons red currant jelly
1 teaspoon brandy
1/4 cup chopped walnuts
1/4 teaspoon aniseed
6–8 sheets edible rice paper
1 3/4 ounces pecorino cheese, thinly
   sliced, to serve

Put all the ingredients except the rice paper and pecorino cheese in a food processor and pulse until the mixture begins to clump together. Transfer to a sheet of waxed paper and, using the paper, roll into a log. Once you have made the log, transfer the log from the waxed paper and wrap in edible rice paper. Store covered in a muslin cloth for several days to allow it to dry out. Slice and serve with pecorino cheese.

pickled nectarines with ricotta and prosciutto

makes 24

3 large nectarines (about 18 ounces)
2/3 cup cider vinegar
2 star anise
2 cloves
1 teaspoon roughly sliced fresh ginger
1 large red chili
1 cup superfine sugar
pinch salt
12 slices prosciutto, cut in half
  lengthwise
1 cup ricotta cheese

Slice the nectarines into quarters, discarding the pits. Put the vinegar, star anise, cloves, ginger, chili, sugar, salt, and 1 1/4 cups of water in a saucepan and bring to a boil. Warm a medium-sized, heatproof, sealable jar by filling it with boiling water, waiting a few minutes, and then draining the water. Put the nectarines in the jar, pour in the boiling vinegar liquid, and seal. Cool, then put in the refrigerator for at least 5 days.

To serve, slice the nectarine quarters in half lengthwise. Lay the prosciutto slices out on a clean work surface and lay one slice of nectarine on top of each. Top with a heaping teaspoon of ricotta cheese, roll up, and serve.

parmesan cookies   makes 65-70

1/2 cup butter, chilled and cubed
1/2 cup grated cheddar cheese
1/2 cup grated Parmesan cheese
1 1/2 cups all-purpose flour
1 teaspoon paprika
1/2 teaspoon salt

Put all the ingredients in a food processor. Using the pulse action, process until the ingredients just combine. Remove the dough and form it into a ball. Divide the dough in half, then roll and shape each portion into a roll about 9 inches long and 1 1/4 inches wide. Roll in waxed paper and chill for 1 hour. The dough can be frozen at this point until ready to use.

Preheat the oven to 350°F. Remove the waxed paper from the dough rolls and cut each portion into 1/4-inch-thick slices. Put on a baking sheet lined with waxed paper and bake for 12–15 minutes, or until pale gold in color. Cool on a wire rack. Repeat until all the cookies are done. Store the cookies in an airtight container until ready to serve.

mashed potatoes

**6 floury potatoes, peeled and cut
  into chunks**
¹/₂ cup milk
7 tablepsoons butter
salt and pepper, to season

Put the potatoes into a large pan of cold salted water and bring to a boil. Cook for about 30 minutes. Put the milk and butter in a small saucepan. Warm over low heat until the butter has melted. When the potato is cooked through, drain and return it to the warm pan. Mash while still warm, then whisk in the buttery milk until the potato is soft and creamy. Season according to taste. Spoon into a warm serving bowl and serve immediately. Serve with roasted chicken or broiled pork sausages.

sweet potato, watercress, and pear salad
serves 4

1 large orange sweet potato
2 tablespoons olive oil
sea salt, to season
1 lemon, juiced
1 tablespoon pink peppercorns,
   drained and finely chopped
3 tablespoons extra-virgin olive oil
2 ripe green pears, quartered and cut
   into bite-sized pieces
2 bunches watercress, sprigs picked

Preheat the oven to 350°F. Peel and cut the sweet potato into bite-sized chunks and put on a baking sheet.

Rub the sweet potato chunks with 2 tablespoons of olive oil and season with sea salt. Bake for 30 minutes, or until they are golden brown and cooked through.

Meanwhile, put the lemon juice, peppercorns, and extra-virgin olive oil in a large bowl and stir to combine. Add the pear pieces and watercress and toss together. Arrange the pear salad on a serving plate and then add the cooked sweet potato.

mashed white beans   serves 4

1 cup cannellini beans
4 garlic cloves
2 teaspoons salt
1/2 cup olive oil
1 tablespoon thyme leaves
sea salt and freshly ground black
   pepper, to season

Soak the cannellini beans overnight. Drain the beans and put them into a saucepan with the garlic. Cover generously with cold water and bring to a boil. Reduce the heat and simmer for 1 hour, or until the beans are soft. Stir in the salt in the last 5 minutes of cooking time. Once the beans are cooked, drain and roughly mash them by hand or put in a food processor with the olive oil and thyme leaves and process until combined. Season to taste with sea salt and freshly ground black pepper. Spoon into a warm serving bowl and serve immediately. Serve with broiled sausages or lamb.

asian-style vegetable salad

dressing

1 teaspoon sambal oelek
1 tablespoon finely chopped
  lemongrass
3 tablespoons lime juice
1 tablespoon jaggery (or brown sugar)
1 tablespoon finely chopped mint

3 1/2 cups trimmed green beans, cut
  in half
1 red bell pepper, julienned
1 cup bean sprouts, trimmed
1 short cucumber, julienned
3 1/4-inch piece daikon radish, peeled
  and finely julienned
1 carrot, peeled and finely julienned
1/4 cup finely chopped roasted peanuts

To make the dressing, put the sambal oelek, lemongrass, lime juice, jaggery, and mint in a small bowl and stir to combine. Set aside.

To make the salad, blanch the green beans in boiling water until they are dark green, then drain and rinse under running cold water. Put them in a bowl with the remaining ingredients, except the peanuts. Toss together. Pour the dressing over the salad, toss, and allow to sit for 15 minutes before serving. Garnish with the peanuts and serve with any simple rice-based Asian-style dish.

sweet couscous

1 cup couscous
1 tablespoon honey
1/2 teaspoon ground cinnamon
1 teaspoon finely grated orange zest
3 tablespoons currants
3 tablespoons toasted flaked almonds
plain yogurt, to serve

Put the couscous in a saucepan with the honey and 2 cups of boiling water. Cover and cook over low heat for 5 minutes, or until all the liquid has been absorbed. Fluff the couscous with a fork, then cover again and remove from the heat. Allow to sit for 10 minutes, then add the cinnamon, orange zest, currants, and almonds. Gently toss to combine and serve with plain yogurt.

mashed butternut squash

serves 4

1 small butternut squash
7 tablespoons butter
1/4 teaspoon ground white pepper
sprinkle of ground cumin
sea salt, to season
extra-virgin olive oil, to drizzle

Peel the squash and cut it into chunks. Put the chunks in a large saucepan of salted cold water and bring to a boil. Boil for 10–12 minutes, or until the squash is cooked through. Drain and return to the pan. Mash while the squash is still warm, then whisk in the butter, white pepper, and ground cumin. Season with sea salt. Spoon into a warm serving bowl and drizzle with extra-virgin olive oil. Serve with broiled lamb or steak.

lemon-braised vegetables

serves 4-6

12 small fingerling potatoes
1 bunch baby carrots, tops trimmed
6 celery sticks, chopped
1/2 cup extra-virgin olive oil
2 lemons, juiced
1 teaspoon sea salt
2 tablespoons finely chopped
  garlic chives

Preheat the oven to 350°F. Scrub the potatoes and carrots and remove any blemishes. If the carrots are too large, cut them in half. Put them in a casserole dish with the celery, olive oil, lemon juice, sea salt, and 1/2 cup of water. Cover and put in the oven for 2 hours. When cooked, scatter with the garlic chives. Serve with roasted chicken or whole baked fish.

mashed celeriac

serves 4

2 medium (about 2¹/₄ pounds)
 celeriac
2 all-purpose potatoes
1 teaspoon lemon juice
2 garlic cloves
3 tablespoons butter
¹/₄ onion, finely diced
¹/₂ cup whipping cream
salt and pepper, to season

Peel the celeriac and potatoes and cut them into chunks. Put the vegetables in a large saucepan of salted cold water with the lemon juice and garlic cloves. Bring to a boil and cook for 25 minutes, or until the celeriac is soft and you can easily pierce it with a knife. Drain the vegetables and return them to the pan. Add the butter and onion. Mash while still warm, slowly adding the cream until the mixture is smooth. Season to taste and serve immediately with broiled steak or seared lamb.

mango salsa

1 large or 2 small mangoes
1 scallion, finely sliced
1 red chili, seeded and finely chopped
2 tablespoons lime juice
sesame oil, to sprinkle
freshly ground black pepper, to season
1 handful cilantro leaves or 4 large
   basil leaves, finely sliced (optional)

Dice the flesh of the mangoes. Put the mango into a bowl with the scallion, chili, lime juice, sesame oil, and some freshly ground black pepper to taste. Toss to combine. If you'd like some herbs in this salsa, add the cilantro or basil leaves. This mango salsa adds a lovely summery taste to barbecued shrimp or chicken.

jeweled couscous

serves 4

15 saffron threads
1 1/2 tablespoons butter
1 cup couscous
1/2 cup currants
1/2 cup slivered almonds, toasted
1/2 cup raw pistachios, toasted
1 orange, zested and juiced
2 tablespoons extra-virgin olive oil
sea salt and freshly ground black
  pepper, to season

Put the saffron threads in a large saucepan with 1/2 cup of water. Put over medium heat and cook until the water has reduced by half. Add the butter and couscous and stir to combine. Add 1 cup of boiling water, cover, and remove from the heat. After about 5 minutes, uncover and fluff the couscous with a fork. Return the lid to the saucepan and allow to sit for an additional 5 minutes.

Put the cooked couscous in a serving bowl and add the currants, almonds, pistachios, and orange zest. Toss together and then stir in the orange juice and olive oil. Season with sea salt and freshly ground black pepper. Serve with roasted chicken.

mango and coconut chutney

serves 4

1 cup dried coconut
1 large green chili, seeded and roughly
   chopped
1 teaspoon finely grated fresh ginger
1 teaspoon lime juice
1/3 cup plain yogurt
1/3 cup finely diced mango
2 tablespoons vegetable oil
2 teaspoons mustard seeds
4 small sprigs curry leaves

Put the coconut, chili, and ginger in a food processor and process to a fine paste. Transfer the mixture to a small bowl and add the lime juice, yogurt, and mango.

In a small frying pan, heat the oil over medium heat and, when hot, add the mustard seeds and curry leaves. When the mustard seeds begin to pop, remove from the heat and spoon the seeds over the coconut mixture. Stir the seeds into the mixture and then spoon the chutney into a small serving bowl. Drain the curry leaves on paper towels and use to garnish the chutney. Serve with barbecued shrimp or chicken.

yorkshire puddings

makes 12 large or 24 mini puddings

1 cup all-purpose flour
1/2 teaspoon salt
2 eggs
1 cup milk

Preheat the oven to 400°F. Sift the flour into a bowl with the salt. Make a well in the center and break the eggs into it. Whisk the mixture together, slowly adding the milk to form a smooth batter. Tip the batter into a pouring jug.

Liberally oil two 6-hole muffin pans (or, for mini puddings, two 12-hole mini muffin pans) and heat the pans in the oven for 15 minutes. Remove from the oven and, working quickly, pour in the batter to half-fill each hole. Return to the oven and bake for 25 minutes. Serve with roast beef and gravy.

marinated artichokes   serves 4

3 lemons, halved
4 globe artichokes
1/4 cup extra-virgin olive oil
8 mint leaves, finely chopped
1 handful Italian parsley leaves,
   roughly chopped
1 garlic clove, crushed
sea salt and freshly ground black
   pepper, to season

Bring a large saucepan of salted water to a boil. Fill a large bowl with cold water and add the juice of 1 lemon. Trim the artichoke stalks to within 3/4 inch of the artichoke head, then pull away the outer leaves until the base of the leaves look yellow and crisp. Use a sharp knife to slice away the top third of the first artichoke and then rub the artichoke with the cut side of a lemon. Place in the water while you repeat the process with the remaining artichokes. Remove the artichokes from the water and scrape out the central choke and pull out any of the spiky inner leaves. Return to the water until ready to cook.

Add the artichokes to the boiling water, weigh them down with a plate, and simmer for about 20 minutes. Test the artichokes by pushing the tip of a knife in just above the stem—it should be tender. Drain, then slice in half.

Put the artichokes in a dish with the olive oil, herbs, garlic, and any remaining lemon juice. Season with sea salt and freshly ground black pepper, and toss to ensure that the artichokes are coated in the marinade.

boiled eggs roasted squash with tahini baked eggs
omelet tofu salad with peanut dressing leek,
saffron, and chickpea soup onion soup poached eggs
soba noodles with ginger broth sweet onion and herb
tart barley and bacon soup soba noodle salad miso
broth with somen noodles, shiitake, and squash
spring chowder crab and tomato tart shiitake mushroom,
squash, and tofu duck and noodle soup quiche lorraine

02   light   meals

tamarind and calamari salad gruyère baked eggs duck
and mango wraps mustard-rubbed tuna salad soba noodle
and herb salad asparagus and fava bean salad
boiled eggs roasted squash with tahini baked eggs
omelet tofu salad with peanut dressing leek, saffron,

boiled eggs

serves 2

2 eggs
salt, freshly ground black pepper, and
buttered toast strips, to serve

Take the eggs from the refrigerator and allow to come to room temperature. Fill a small saucepan with enough cold water to cover the eggs and bring it to a boil over high heat. When it has reached boiling point, reduce the heat to a rolling boil. Using a spoon, lower the eggs, one at a time, into the water. Boil for 5 minutes, then remove. If you prefer your eggs set firmly, cook for an additional 1 minute. Perch each egg in an egg cup and, with a sharp knife, carefully crack off the top. Serve with salt, freshly ground black pepper, and buttered toast strips.

roasted squash with tahini

serves 4

1 small butternut squash
1 tablespoon oil
sea salt and freshly ground black
  pepper, to season
3 tablespoons tahini
1/2 cup plain yogurt
1 teaspoon ground roasted cumin
1/2 teaspoon finely chopped garlic
1 tablespoon lemon juice
31/2 cups arugula
1 large handful Italian parsley leaves
1 tablespoon black sesame seeds

Preheat the oven to 350°F. Peel the butternut squash and cut it into large chunks. Toss it in the oil, season with salt and freshly ground black pepper, and then put the chunks on a baking sheet. Roast for 30 minutes, or until the butternut squash is tender, then allow it to cool.

To make the dressing, mix the tahini, yogurt, cumin, garlic, and lemon juice to a smooth paste and then season with sea salt and freshly ground black pepper to taste.

Toss the arugula and parsley leaves together and pile them onto a serving plate. Top with the roasted squash, add a spoonful of the dressing, and garnish with a sprinkling of sesame seeds.

baked eggs

4 eggs
1 tablespoon finely snipped chives
**2 tablespoons finely grated Parmesan
  cheese**
**sea salt and ground white pepper, to
  season**

Preheat the oven to 350°F. Generously grease two 3¼-inch ramekins and put them in a roasting pan half-filled with water. Put the eggs in a small bowl and add the snipped chives and Parmesan cheese. Whisk together and season with sea salt and ground white pepper. Divide the egg mixture between the two ramekins and bake for 15 minutes, or until the egg is cooked through. Serve with toast.

omelet

3 eggs
1¹/₂ tablespoons butter
baby spinach leaves
chives, snipped, to garnish

Separate the eggs. Whisk the egg whites until they form soft peaks, then lightly fold the egg yolks and whites together.

Heat a 10-inch nonstick frying pan over medium heat and add the butter. When the butter has melted and begins to sizzle, add the egg mixture. Using a spatula, fold the edges of the omelet into the center as it cooks.

When the omelet is nearly cooked, flip one side over the other and remove the pan from the heat. Gently slide the cooked omelet onto a plate. Serve with the baby spinach on the side and garnish with a sprinkling of snipped chives.

tofu salad with peanut dressing

serves 4

1 tablespoon shaved jaggery (or brown sugar)

1 tablespoon balsamic vinegar

2 tablespoons kecap manis

1 red chili, seeded and finely chopped

1 garlic clove, finely chopped

1/2 cup roasted and ground peanuts

1 2/3 cups firm tofu (about 10 1/2 ounces)

1/2 cup rice flour

sea salt and freshly ground black pepper, to season

1 1/4 cups peanut oil

2 cups watercress sprigs

1 cup bean sprouts, trimmed

To make the dressing, combine the jaggery, vinegar, kecap manis, and 5 tablespoons of boiling water in a small bowl. Stir until the jaggery has dissolved. Add the chili, garlic, and peanuts. Set aside.

Drain the tofu on paper towels and cut into small cubes. Put the rice flour in a plastic bag with a little sea salt and freshly ground black pepper. Add the tofu and toss until well coated. Heat a frying pan over high heat and add the peanut oil. Deep-fry a few tofu cubes at a time until they are golden brown, then remove with a slotted spoon and drain on paper towels.

To assemble the salad, arrange the watercress and bean sprouts on four plates and top with the tofu. Drizzle with the dressing.

leek, saffron, and chickpea soup

serves 4

3 tablespoons butter
15 saffron threads
3 leeks, white part only, finely diced
1 lemon, zest peeled into thick strips
1 carrot, peeled and grated
3 tablespoons roughly chopped
  Italian parsley
4 cups chicken stock (see basics)
2$^1/_2$ cups drained and rinsed canned
  chickpeas

Heat the butter and saffron threads in a large saucepan over medium heat. Add the leeks when the butter begins to bubble, and cook until they are soft and transparent. Add the lemon zest, carrot, and parsley, and cook for an additional minute before adding the stock and chickpeas. Bring to a boil, then reduce the heat and simmer for an additional 15 minutes. Serve hot.

onion soup

3 tablespoons butter
8 medium brown onions, peeled and
  finely sliced
2 garlic cloves
1 tablespoon finely chopped rosemary
4 cups chicken stock (see basics)
sea salt and ground white pepper, to
  season
1 cup roughly chopped Italian parsley
2/3 cup grated vintage cheddar cheese

Melt the butter in a large saucepan over medium heat and then add the onions, garlic, and rosemary. Cover and allow the onions to slowly sauté, stirring occasionally until they are soft and have almost dissolved. This will take about half an hour.

Add the chicken stock, season with sea salt and ground white pepper, and continue to cook for another half hour. To serve, divide the soup between four large soup bowls and sprinkle with the parsley and cheddar cheese. Serve immediately.

poached eggs

1 teaspoon white wine vinegar
1 egg
whole-wheat toast, to serve

For great poached eggs, really fresh eggs are essential. Fill a deep frying pan with about 2 inches of cold water. Add the white wine vinegar and bring to a simmering boil. Crack an egg into a saucer and gently lower the egg into the water. Lower the heat and cook for 5 minutes. Remove the egg with a slotted spoon and drain on a paper towel. Serve with whole-wheat toast.

soba noodles
with ginger broth

serves 4

14 ounces soba noodles
4 cups chicken stock (see basics)
1 tablespoon finely grated fresh ginger
2 teaspoons soy sauce
1 teaspoon fish sauce
3 scallions, finely sliced
1 1/3 cups cubed fresh soft tofu

Bring a large pot of water to a boil and cook the soba noodles until they are al dente. Drain and rinse under cold running water and set aside. Put the chicken stock, ginger, soy sauce, and fish sauce in a saucepan and bring to a boil. Reduce the heat to low and simmer for 5 minutes.

Divide the noodles between four bowls and top with the scallions and tofu. Ladle the hot broth over the soba noodles and serve immediately.

sweet onion and herb tart

serves 6

2 tablespoons butter
1/2 teaspoon finely chopped rosemary
1/2 teaspoon finely chopped thyme
13/4 pounds brown onions, finely sliced
1/2 cup white wine
1 prebaked 10-inch short-crust tart
   shell (see basics)
1 cup heavy cream
4 egg yolks
sea salt and freshly ground black
   pepper, to season
1/2 cup grated Gruyère cheese

Preheat the oven to 350°F. Using a large frying pan (with a lid), melt the butter over medium heat along with the rosemary and thyme. Add the onions and sauté until the onion is soft and transparent. Add the white wine and cover the pan. Reduce the heat to low and gently simmer for about 40 minutes, or until the onion is richly caramelized. Spread the onion mixture into the tart shell.

Put the cream and egg yolks in a bowl and whisk together. Season with sea salt and freshly ground black pepper and stir in the Gruyère cheese. Pour the cream mixture over the onion mixture and carefully put the tart in the oven. Bake for 30 minutes, or until the filling has set and is lightly golden. Serve with a bitter leaf salad.

barley and bacon soup serves 4

3 tablespoons butter
2 garlic cloves, finely chopped
3 leeks, white part only, washed and
  finely chopped
1 teaspoon thyme leaves
1/2 teaspoon finely chopped rosemary
4 slices bacon, finely diced
1 large carrot, grated
2 celery sticks, finely sliced
3/4 cup pearl barley
8 cups chicken or vegetable stock
  (see basics)
1 handful Italian parsley leaves
1/2 cup grated Parmesan cheese

Melt the butter in a large saucepan over medium heat and add the garlic and leeks. Stir for 1 minute before adding the thyme, rosemary, and bacon. Continue to cook until the leeks are soft and transparent. Add the carrot, celery, and barley, and cook for an additional 5 minutes, stirring. Pour in the stock, cover with a lid, and reduce the heat to a simmer. Cook for 1 hour, or until the barley is soft.

Ladle the hot soup into four bowls and top with the parsley and Parmesan.

soba noodle salad   serves 4

4 tablespoons arame or hijiki seaweed
1 teaspoon dashi granules
1/2 cup soy sauce
1/4 cup mirin
1 teaspoon sugar
1 tablespoon pickled ginger, finely
   chopped
4 scallions, finely sliced on the
   diagonal
10 1/2 ounces soba noodles
12-inch piece daikon, julienned
1 short cucumber, julienned
20 mint leaves, roughly torn

Soak the arame or hijiki in warm water for 30 minutes and then drain it. Combine the dashi granules, soy sauce, mirin, and sugar with 1 1/2 cups of water in a small saucepan and bring to a boil, stirring so that the sugar dissolves. Remove the pan from the heat and allow the sauce to cool. Add the pickled ginger and scallions.

Cook the noodles in a pot of boiling water until they are al dente, then drain and rinse with cold water to remove any starch.

Toss the noodles, daikon, seaweed, cucumber, mint, and sauce together and divide between four bowls. Serve the salad as is, or top it with a small piece of teriyaki salmon.

miso broth with somen noodles, shiitake, and squash

serves 4

6 dried shiitake mushrooms
1 teaspoon dashi granules
3 tablespoons miso paste
2 tablespoons soy sauce
2 cups peeled and cubed winter
    squash
7 ounces somen noodles
2 scallions, sliced on the diagonal

Cover the shiitake mushrooms with 2 cups of hot water and soak for about 30 minutes. Remove and finely slice the mushrooms, reserving the soaking liquid.

Put the dashi granules, 4 cups of water, the reserved mushroom liquid, miso paste, soy sauce, mushrooms, and squash in a large saucepan and bring to a boil. Reduce the heat and simmer for 10 minutes.

Bring a large pot of water to a boil and cook the noodles for 3 minutes. Drain, rinse, and divide among four warm bowls. Spoon the miso soup over the somen noodles and top with the sliced scallions.

spring chowder

serves 4

3 1/4 pounds cleaned clams
1 tablespoon light olive oil
1 garlic clove, crushed
2 slices bacon, chopped
2 onions, diced
1 red chili, seeded and finely chopped
1 carrot, grated
1 bay leaf
2 large all-purpose potatoes, peeled
   and diced
2 celery sticks, thinly sliced
1 cup roughly chopped Italian parsley
sea salt and white pepper, to season

Throw away any clams that don't close when you tap them. Bring 2 cups of water to a boil in a large saucepan, add the clams, then cover and cook for 2–3 minutes until they open. Discard any that stay closed. Take most of the clams out of their shells, keeping some whole for the garnish. Strain and reserve the clam cooking liquid.

Put the olive oil, garlic, and bacon in the saucepan and cook over medium heat until the bacon has browned. Add the onions, chili, carrot, and bay leaf. When the onion is translucent, tip in the potatoes, clam liquid, and 1 cup of water. Cover and simmer for about 35 minutes. Add the celery, clams, and parsley. Season with sea salt and white pepper. Ladle the chowder into four soup bowls and garnish with the whole clams.

crab and tomato tart   serves 6

10 saffron threads
1 cup heavy cream
4 egg yolks
sea salt and freshly ground black
   pepper, to season
3 tablespoons finely snipped chives
2 ripe plum tomatoes, finely chopped
1 prebaked 10-inch short-crust tart
   shell (see basics)
1 cup fresh crabmeat, shredded

Preheat the oven to 350°F. Put the saffron threads in a small saucepan with 4 tablespoons of cold water. Place over high heat and simmer until the liquid has reduced to about 1 tablespoon. Remove from the heat and add the cream. Stir to combine, then whisk in the egg yolks. Season with sea salt and freshly ground black pepper, then add the chives. Sprinkle the tomato in the prebaked tart shell. Sprinkle the crabmeat over the tomato. Pour the cream mixture over the top. Bake the tart for about 25 minutes, or until the filling has set and is lightly golden. Serve with a watercress salad.

shiitake mushroom, squash, and tofu

serves 2

6 dried shiitake mushrooms

3/4-inch piece fresh ginger, peeled and cut into thin strips

6-inch piece daikon, peeled and cut into 1/2-inch rounds

1 carrot, peeled and cut into 1/2-inch rounds

1/2 small butternut squash, peeled and cut into large chunks

12/3 cups silken firm tofu, at room temperature

Cover the shiitake mushrooms with 2 cups of hot water and soak for about 30 minutes. Remove the mushrooms and trim off any tough stems. Put the mushrooms in a pan along with the strained soaking liquid and add the ginger, daikon, and carrot. Bring to a boil, then reduce the heat and simmer for 10 minutes. Add the squash and gently simmer, covered, for an additional 20–25 minutes.

Cut the tofu into large chunks and divide between two warmed bowls. Using the point of a sharp knife, check that the squash is cooked through, then spoon the ingredients and stock into the bowls and serve.

duck and noodle soup serves 4

2 duck breasts, trimmed, reserving
  excess fat
8 scallions, sliced into 1¼-inch lengths
9 ounces soba noodles
6 cups dashi stock (see basics)
4 tablespoons soy sauce
1 tablespoon sugar

Finely slice the meat across the duck breast in ¼-inch thick slices. Heat the duck fat in a small frying pan, add the sliced scallions, and sauté lightly, then set aside.

Cook the noodles in a large pot of boiling water, then drain and set aside. Combine the dashi stock, soy sauce, and sugar in a saucepan and bring to a boil. Reduce the heat and simmer for 10 minutes. Add the sliced duck and cook for an additional minute.

Divide the noodles among four warmed bowls. Top the noodles with the duck meat and sautéed scallion. Ladle the hot duck broth into each bowl and serve immediately.

quiche lorraine   serves 6

1 teaspoon butter
6 slices bacon, finely chopped
2 eggs
2 egg yolks
1 cup heavy cream
sea salt and white pepper, to season
1 cup grated Parmesan cheese
1 prebaked 10-inch tart shell (see
    basics)

Preheat the oven to 350°F. Melt the butter in a heavy-based frying pan over medium heat. Add the bacon and cook until lightly brown and crisp. Remove with a slotted spoon and drain on paper towels.

Put the eggs, egg yolks, and cream in a bowl and whisk together. Season with sea salt and white pepper, then stir in the Parmesan cheese. Sprinkle the bacon into the prebaked tart shell and pour the egg mixture over. Carefully put the tart in the oven and bake for 25 minutes, or until the filling is set and the top is golden brown. Serve with a green salad.

tamarind and calamari salad

serves 4

1 tablespoon tamarind concentrate
1 tablespoon sugar
2 tablespoons fish sauce
1 tablespoon lime juice
1 garlic clove, crushed
1 small red chili, seeded and julienned
4 medium squid (about 14 ounces),
  cleaned
3 tablespoons oil
1/2 cup basil leaves
1/2 cup cilantro leaves
1 cup bean sprouts

To make the dressing, blend the tamarind with 1/4 cup of warm water. Add the sugar, fish sauce, lime juice, garlic, and chili, and stir until the sugar has dissolved.

Rinse the squid under cold running water and pat it dry with paper towels. Cut the tubes open down one side and lightly score the outside surface with crisscross marks—this will make it curl up when you cook it. Heat the oil in a frying pan over high heat and fry the squid tubes for 3–4 minutes on each side.

Cut each tube into bite-sized pieces and toss them in the dressing with the herbs and sprouts. Serve with rice noodles or steamed white rice.

gruyère baked eggs

makes 4

3 tablespoons butter, softened
4 slices prosciutto, finely chopped
4 tablespoons finely chopped Italian
  parsley
8 eggs
salt and freshly ground black pepper,
  to season
2 tablespoons grated Gruyère cheese
toast, to serve

Preheat the oven to 350°F. Generously butter four 3 1/4-inch ramekins and put them in a roasting pan half-filled with cold water.

Divide the prosciutto and parsley between the ramekins. Put the eggs in a bowl, season with salt and freshly ground black pepper, and then lightly whisk them together. Fill the ramekins with the egg mixture, sprinkle with the cheese, and put the roasting pan in the oven. Bake for 25–30 minutes, by which time the egg should be just set. Serve with toast.

duck and mango wraps   serves 4

1 teaspoon Szechuan peppercorns
1 teaspoon black peppercorns
1/2 teaspoon sea salt
1/2 Chinese roasted duck
8 round rice paper wrappers
4 tablespoons plum sauce (see basics)
2 ripe mangoes, peeled and sliced
1 cup snow-pea shoots

Put both types of peppercorn and the sea salt in a spice grinder and grind to form a coarse seasoning. Set aside.

Remove the skin from the duck and slice it into thin strips with a pair of clean kitchen scissors. Remove the flesh and shred it.

Soak the rice paper wrappers, one at a time, in hot water until they become soft, then remove and pat dry.

Put some of the plum sauce along the center of a softened wrapper and top with some duck flesh, duck skin, sliced mango, snow-pea shoots, and a sprinkle of the pepper seasoning. Roll up, folding in the sides to make a neat wrap. When ready to serve, cut the duck wraps in half and arrange on a serving platter.

mustard-rubbed tuna salad

serves 4

1 teaspoon ground white pepper
1 tablespoon Dijon mustard
3 tablespoons olive oil
14-ounce tuna fillet, cut into 3/4-inch-
   wide strips
2 bunches watercress, leaves picked
2 1/2 cups chervil, trimmed
2 small zucchini, finely sliced
4 red radishes, finely sliced
1/2 cup lemon mayonnaise (see basics)

Mix the white pepper, Dijon mustard, and 1 tablespoon of olive oil together in a small bowl. Rub the mustard mixture all over the tuna.

Add the remaining olive oil to a large nonstick frying pan and heat over high heat. Sear the tuna for 1 minute on each side. Remove from the heat and allow to rest. Divide the watercress, chervil, zucchini, and radish between four plates.

Cut the tuna fillet into thin slices and arrange over the salad. Top with a dollop of lemon mayonnaise.

soba noodle
and herb salad

serves 4

3 tablespoons soy sauce

3 tablespoons sesame oil

1½ tablespoons Chinese black vinegar

3 tablespoons grated jaggery (or brown
sugar)

3 tablespoons lime juice

1 tablespoon finely chopped
lemongrass, white part only

1 red chili, seeded and finely chopped

10½ ounces soba noodles

2-inch piece fresh ginger, peeled and
finely julienned

1 bunch mint

1 bunch cilantro

4½-inch piece daikon, peeled and
julienned

Put the soy sauce, sesame oil,
vinegar, sugar, lime juice, lemongrass,
and chili in a large bowl and stir until
the sugar has dissolved.

Bring a large pot of water to a boil
and cook the soba noodles until al
dente, then drain and rinse them
under cold running water. Put them in
the bowl with the dressing and toss to
coat. Add the ginger, mint, cilantro,
and daikon to the noodles, toss
together, then pile into four bowls and
serve.

asparagus and fava bean salad

3 tablespoons extra-virgin olive oil
1 tablespoon lemon juice
sea salt and freshly ground black
   pepper, to season
2 bunches asparagus, trimmed
1 3/4 cups fava beans
2/3 cup goat cheese
1 handful Italian parsley

Bring a large pot of salted water to a boil. Put the olive oil and lemon juice in a large bowl and season with sea salt and freshly ground black pepper. Add the asparagus to the boiling water and cook for 2–3 minutes, until bright green. Remove from the water with tongs and rinse under cold running water. Don't discard the water.

Put the asparagus in the bowl with the lemon juice and oil and toss so that the asparagus is well coated in the dressing. Add the fava beans to the boiling water and cook for 5 minutes. Drain and remove the tough outer skin. Divide the asparagus between four plates and sprinkle with the fava beans. Top with the goat cheese and parsley leaves, and drizzle with any of the leftover dressing.

leek and lemon fettucine whole baked fish salmon
with lemongrass and black vinegar dressing leek and
squash risotto roasted squash and onions on couscous
with harissa braised mushrooms with buttered angel-
hair pasta cod with white pepper and lemon sauce
roasted lamb couscous with herbs and chickpeas somen
noodles with seared shrimp zucchini and thyme
risotto snapper with citrus dressing tuna salad with

03   main   meals

fried lemon zest hokkien noodle stir-fry lemon thyme
roasted chicken pan-fried fish with lemon and black
bean sauce lemon pasta seared lime salmon with poppy
seeds aromatic noodles with seared salmon steamed
fish with fresh ginger lemon and saffron risotto

leek and lemon fettucine

serves 4

3 tablespoons olive oil
3 garlic cloves, crushed
1 tablespoon oregano leaves
3 large leeks, white part only, finely
  sliced
sea salt and freshly ground black
  pepper, to seaon
14 ounces fettucine
1 lemon, zest grated
1 tablespoon small capers
3/4 cup grated Parmesan cheese, plus
  extra to serve
1 cup roughly chopped Italian parsley

Bring a large saucepan of water to a boil for the pasta. Heat the olive oil in a large frying pan over medium heat, then add the garlic, oregano, and leeks. Sauté until the leeks are soft and transparent, then season with sea salt and freshly ground black pepper.

Cook the pasta until it is al dente, then drain and return it to the warm pan. Add the leeks, grated lemon zest, capers, Parmesan cheese, and parsley, stirring them into the pasta. Season with salt and freshly ground black pepper, then serve with extra Parmesan cheese.

whole baked fish

serves 4

2 lemongrass stems, white part only,
roughly chopped, plus 1 finely sliced
1 large piece of ginger, thickly sliced
3 scallions, cut into 1½-inch lengths
1 cup white wine
3¼-pound whole snapper or other firm
whitefish
sea salt, for rubbing
1 lemon, thickly sliced, plus extra
wedges, to serve
2 tablespoons olive oil

Put the chopped lemongrass stems,
ginger, and scallions in a roasting pan.
Pour the white wine over.

Rinse the fish under cold running
water and pat dry with paper towels.
Using a sharp knife, cut the fish skin in
a crisscross pattern. Rub the fish with
a little sea salt and put it in the
roasting pan. Put the extra finely sliced
lemongrass stem and the sliced
lemon into the fish cavity. Drizzle the
fish with olive oil and bake for 35–40
minutes. Serve with lemon wedges.

salmon with lemongrass and black vinegar dressing

serves 4

lemongrass and black vinegar dressing
1 lemongrass stem
1 tablespoon finely grated fresh ginger
1/2 cup mirin
2 tablespoons Chinese black vinegar

1 bunch spinach (about 18 ounces),
   washed and trimmed
4 scallions, trimmed and cut into
   1 1/4-inch lengths
four 6-ounce salmon fillets
freshly ground black pepper, to season

To make the lemongrass and black vinegar dressing, trim the lemongrass stem of its tough outer leaves and base. Slice the stem in half lengthwise and finely chop the tender bottom part of the stem. Put it in a small bowl with the ginger, mirin, and vinegar.

Put the spinach leaves and scallions in a frying pan. Add 1 cup of water and top with the salmon. Put the pan over high heat and cover so that the water begins to steam the spinach. Cook for 8 minutes.

Remove the salmon carefully and put onto warmed plates with the spinach and scallions. Spoon the black vinegar dressing over the salmon and spinach. Season with freshly ground black pepper.

leek and squash risotto

serves 4

4 cups chicken or vegetable stock
(see basics)
3 tablespoons butter
2 garlic cloves, finely chopped
2 leeks, white part only, finely sliced
1 cup arborio (risotto) rice
4 1/2 cups peeled and finely diced
winter squash
4 tablespoons grated Parmesan
cheese, plus extra to serve
olive oil, to drizzle

Heat the stock in a saucepan. In another heavy-based saucepan, heat the butter over medium heat. Add the garlic and leeks. Sauté until the leek is soft. Add the rice and stir for 1 minute, or until the grains are well coated and glossy. Add 1 cup of stock, simmer, and stir until absorbed. Add the diced squash and another 1 cup of stock, and stir until absorbed. Add another 1 cup of stock, stir until absorbed, then test if the rice is al dente. If the rice is not quite cooked, add the remaining stock and simmer until it has reduced and the rice is coated in a creamy sauce. Fold the Parmesan cheese through.

Spoon into bowls and sprinkle with more cheese. Garnish with a drizzle of olive oil.

roasted squash and onions on couscous with harissa

serves 4

13/4 pounds winter squash, cut into
　large bite-sized pieces
6 small scallions, trimmed and halved
2 tablespoons extra-virgin olive oil
sea salt and freslhy ground black
　pepper, to season
1 cup couscous
11/2 tablespoons butter
1 cup baby spinach leaves
harissa (see basics)

Preheat the oven to 400°F. Put the squash pieces and scallions in a roasting pan. Drizzle with olive oil and season with sea salt and freshly ground black pepper. Bake for about 20 minutes. Remove from the oven and turn the vegetables over. Return to the oven and bake for an additional 20 minutes.

In a bowl, cover the couscous with 11/2 cups boiling water and add the butter. Cover the bowl and allow to sit for 5 minutes. Fluff the couscous with a fork and then spoon onto four plates. Top with the spinach leaves, squash, and scallions, then spoon the harissa over the top.

braised mushrooms with buttered angel-hair pasta

serves 4

1¹/₂ pounds mixed mushrooms (button,
   cremini, shiitake, oyster, and enoki)
3 tablespoons olive oil
3 garlic cloves, crushed
1 tablespoon thyme leaves
1 cup white wine
sea salt, to season
9 ounces fresh angel-hair pasta or
   dried linguine
3 tablespoons butter
2 tablespoons finely chopped Italian
   parsley
freshly ground black pepper, to season
4 tablespoons finely grated Parmesan
   cheese

Bring a large pot of salted water to a boil. Slice the mushrooms into halves or quarters. Heat the oil in a large saucepan over medium heat and add the garlic, mushrooms, and thyme. Toss the mushrooms in the pan and cook until the garlic begins to soften. Add the white wine and season with sea salt. Cover with a lid and simmer for 7 minutes.

Add the pasta to the boiling water and cook until al dente. Drain the pasta, then put it back in the warm pot. Stir the butter and parsley through the pasta, then pile it onto four warmed plates. Make a well in the center of the pasta and fill with the mushrooms. Drizzle with the mushroom cooking liquid and season with freshly ground black pepper. Serve sprinkled with the Parmesan cheese.

cod with white pepper and lemon sauce

serves 4

2 lemons, juiced
1 teaspoon ground white pepper
1 teaspoon superfine sugar
four 7-ounce cod or other firm
  whitefish fillets
2 tablespoons olive oil
3 tomatoes, roughly chopped
12 basil leaves

To make the white pepper and lemon sauce, put the lemon juice, white pepper, and sugar in a small bowl and stir until the sugar has dissolved. Rinse the fish fillets in cold water and dry on paper towels.

Heat the olive oil in a large nonstick frying pan over high heat. Add the fish fillets and cook for 2 minutes on one side. Turn the fish over and reduce the heat to low–medium. Cook for an additional 3–4 minutes.

Toss the tomatoes and basil together and divide between four plates. Arrange the fish over the top and spoon the dressing over. Serve with an arugula salad.

roasted lamb

serves 6

3¹/₄-pound leg of lamb
olive oil
salt and freshly ground black pepper,
  for rubbing
5 garlic cloves, halved
6 rosemary sprigs

Preheat the oven to 400°F. With the point of a small, sharp knife, make several incisions into the skin of the leg of lamb. Rub the surface of the lamb with a little olive oil, then rub salt and freshly ground black pepper into the skin. Press the garlic into the incisions. Sprinkle rosemary over the base of a roasting pan and put the lamb on top.

Bake for 30 minutes, then spoon some of the juices from the pan over the lamb. Bake for 40 minutes more. Transfer the lamb to a warm platter, cover with aluminum foil, and let it rest for 15 minutes before carving. Serve with roasted vegetables.

couscous with herbs and chickpeas

serves 4

1 cup couscous

1 teaspoon butter

1 3/4 cups canned chickpeas, drained and rinsed

2 plum tomatoes, seeded and diced

1/2 red onion, finely diced

1 large handful mint leaves

1 large handful cilantro leaves

1 large handful Italian parsley leaves

1 tablespoon lemon juice

3 tablespoons olive oil

2 tablespoons diced preserved lemon rind

sea salt and freshly ground black pepper, to season

Put the couscous in a large bowl with the butter and cover with 1 cup of boiling water. Leave the couscous for 20–30 minutes, occasionally separating the grains with a fork. Rub the grains between your fingers to break up any lumps, then add the remaining salad ingredients.

Toss the couscous and salad together and season with sea salt and freshly ground black pepper.

somen noodles with seared shrimp

serves 4

3 tablespoons rice vinegar

1 teaspoon finely grated fresh ginger

1/4 cup sweet mirin

1 tablespoon tamari

51/2 ounces somen noodles

1 tablespoon olive oil

16 large raw shrimp, peeled and deveined with tails intact

2 short cucumbers, finely julienned

2/3 cup finely snipped chives

2 tablespoons raw sesame seeds

1 teaspoon red chili flakes

Put the rice vinegar, ginger, mirin, and tamari in a small bowl and stir to combine. Set aside.

In a pot of boiling water, cook the noodles until they are al dente. Drain and rinse the noodles and set aside.

Heat a nonstick frying pan over high heat and add the olive oil. Sear the shrimp on both sides for 2–3 minutes, or until they are pink and beginning to curl up. Put the noodles in a bowl with the dressing, cucumber, and chives. Stir to combine, then divide between four serving bowls. Top with the seared shrimp.

Put the sesame seeds and chili flakes in a shallow saucepan and cook over medium heat, stirring lightly, until the seeds begin to turn golden brown. Spoon the warm seeds over the top of the shrimp and drizzle with any remaining dressing.

zucchini and thyme risotto

serves 4

4 cups chicken or vegetable stock
 (see basics)
4 1/2 tablespoons butter
2 garlic cloves, chopped
1 onion, finely diced
3 zucchini, finely diced
1 tablespoon thyme
1 cup arborio (risotto) rice
1 cup white wine
3/4 cup grated Parmesan cheese
goat cheese, to serve
drizzle of olive oil, to serve

Heat the chicken or vegetable stock in a saucepan. Heat 1 tablespoon of the butter in a large frying pan over medium heat, then add the garlic, onion, and zucchini. Sauté until soft and then set aside.

Heat 2 tablespoons of butter and the thyme in a heavy-based saucepan over medium heat. Add the rice and stir for 1 minute, or until the grains are coated. Add the wine, simmer, and stir until absorbed. Add 1 cup of stock and stir until absorbed. Stir in another 1 cup of stock. When almost fully absorbed, stir in the zucchini. Test if the rice is al dente. If undercooked, add the remaining stock and simmer until the stock has reduced and the rice is coated with the sauce. Fold the Parmesan cheese through. Spoon into four bowls. Garnish with goat cheese and a drizzle of olive oil.

snapper with citrus dressing

2 oranges

1 lemon

2 limes

1/2 teaspoon pink peppercorns, roughly
  chopped

4 tablespoons light olive oil

2 tablespoons vegetable oil

four 7-ounce snapper or other firm
  whitefish fillets, skin on

sea salt, to season

Preheat the oven to 400°F. To make the dressing, zest the oranges, lemon, and limes, and put the zest in a bowl. Juice the lemon and add the juice to the bowl. Segment the oranges and limes, and put them in the bowl along with any juice, then add the peppercorns and light olive oil and stir well.

Put the vegetable oil in a large ovenproof frying pan over high heat. Rinse the snapper fillets in cold water and pat them dry with paper towels. Season the fillets liberally with sea salt and put them skin side down in the hot pan. Sear the fillets for a minute or two, or until the skin is crisp and golden, and then turn them over.

Put the pan into the oven and bake for 8 minutes, then transfer the fillets to a serving dish. Spoon the dressing over the fish and serve immediately.

tuna salad with fried lemon zest

serves 4

four 7-ounce tuna steaks
5 tablespoons olive oil
1 tablespoon lemon juice
1 tablespoon lemon thyme leaves
2 handfuls baby arugula leaves
2 handfuls radicchio leaves
2 handfuls mizuna leaves
2 cups cherry tomatoes, halved
1/2 cup small black olives
1 long cucumber, peeled and seeded
2 lemons
1 handful Italian parsley
extra-virgin olive oil, to serve
lemon wedges, to serve

Cut the tuna steaks into several large pieces and cover with 3 tablespoons of the olive oil and all the lemon juice and thyme. Allow to marinate for several hours.

Put the salad leaves, cherry tomatoes, and olives on a serving platter. Cut the cucumber into bite-sized chunks and add to the salad.

Remove the zest from 2 lemons with a vegetable peeler and cut into thin strips. Heat the remaining olive oil in a small frying pan over medium heat. Cook the zest for 3 minutes, removing it as it begins to turn golden brown. Drain on paper towels.

Heat a nonstick frying pan or broiler and sear the tuna for 1 minute on all sides. Arrange the tuna over the salad and sprinkle with the fried lemon zest and parsley leaves. Drizzle with a little extra-virgin olive oil and serve with lemon wedges.

hokkien noodle stir-fry

serves 4

1 bunch bok choy (about 1¼ pounds)
1 long cucumber
1 tablespoon peanut oil
2 garlic cloves, finely chopped
2 large red chilies, seeded and finely
  sliced
1 tablespoon grated fresh ginger
1 red onion, sliced
1 red bell pepper, finely sliced
1 pound fresh Hokkien noodles
3 tablespoons kecap manis
1 tablespoon black sesame seeds,
  to serve

Rinse the bok choy and slice it into halves or quarters, depending on its size. Peel the cucumber, slice it in half lengthwise, and, using a teaspoon, remove the seeds, then cut the halves into thick slices diagonally.

Heat the peanut oil in a wok over medium heat and add the garlic, chilies, ginger, and onion. Stir-fry until the onion is soft, then remove and set aside. Add the bok choy, cucumber, and bell pepper to the wok and stir-fry until the bok choy is soft and wilted. Remove and set aside. Add the noodles and kecap manis and stir-fry until the noodles are heated through. Return the vegetables to the wok and stir-fry for 1 minute. Divide among four plates and sprinkle with the black sesame seeds.

lemon thyme roasted chicken

1 whole 4-pound chicken
1 bunch lemon thyme
salt, for rubbing
3 lemons, halved
1 onion, quartered
3 tablespoons butter, softened

Preheat the oven to 400°F. Rinse the chicken well and pat it dry with paper towels. Scatter some of the lemon thyme over the base of a roasting pan, then generously rub the chicken skin with salt and put it on top of the lemon thyme, breast side up.

Put two lemon halves inside the chicken along with the onion quarters and some lemon thyme. Rub the softened butter over the breast meat. Cook the chicken for 1 hour 15 minutes, or until it is cooked through. Take the chicken out of the oven and check that it is cooked by pulling a leg away from the body—the juices that run out should be clear and not pink.

Squeeze the two remaining lemons over the chicken and cook for an additional 5 minutes. Remove the chicken from the oven and let it rest for 10 minutes before carving. Arrange the chicken pieces on a serving platter and pour some of the lemony pan juices over them.

pan-fried fish with lemon and black bean sauce

serves 4

1 tablespoon olive oil
2 scallions, trimmed and finely sliced
1 red bell pepper, finely diced
2 tablespoons salted black beans,
   rinsed and drained
1 cup fish stock (see basics)
1 lemon, juiced
1 tablespoon all-purpose flour
1/2 teaspoon sea salt
freshly ground black pepper, to season
four 6-ounce firm whitefish fillets
1/2 cup peanut oil

To make the lemon and black bean sauce, heat the oil in a frying pan over medium heat and add the scallions and bell pepper. Cook for 5 minutes, or until the bell pepper is soft.

Add the black beans and stock and cook until reduced by half. Stir the lemon juice through, then pour into a small bowl. Clean the pan by wiping it with paper towels.

Put the flour in a plastic bag with the sea salt and freshly ground black pepper. Add the fish fillets and toss until they are lightly coated with flour. Heat the peanut oil in the frying pan over high heat. Add the fish and cook for 2 minutes, then turn the fish over and reduce the heat to medium. Cook for an additional 5 minutes. Put the fish on a serving plate and spoon over the sauce. Serve with steamed greens and rice.

lemon pasta

3 tablespoons extra-virgin olive oil
15 basil leaves, finely sliced
3 tablespoons roughly chopped
  Italian parsley
2 garlic cloves, finely chopped
2 lemons, zested and juiced
18 ounces tubular pasta, such as
  casareccia
3/4 cup finely grated Parmesan cheese
sea salt and freshly ground black
  pepper, to season

Bring a large pot of salted water to a boil. Put the olive oil, basil, parsley, garlic, and lemon zest and juice in a bowl and stir to combine. Add the pasta to the boiling water and cook until al dente. Drain the pasta and return it to the warm pot. Add the lemon and herb oil and stir the pasta until it is coated. Add the Parmesan cheese and stir again. Season with sea salt and freshly ground black pepper.

seared lime salmon
with poppy seeds
serves 4

four 6-ounce salmon fillets, skin on
3 limes
1 tablespoon soy sauce
3 tablespoons olive oil
3 tablespoons mirin
1 tablespoon poppy seeds, to serve
steamed rice, to serve

Preheat the broiler. Rinse the salmon fillets in cold water and pat them dry with paper towels. Put the salmon in a bowl and add the juice of two of the limes, the soy sauce, and the olive oil. Leave to marinate for half an hour. Remove the skin from the remaining lime and slice the flesh into paper-thin circles. Heat a large nonstick frying pan over high heat and sear the salmon, skin side up, for 1 minute. Turn the fillets over and take the pan off the heat.

Top the salmon fillets with the sliced lime and spoon over the mirin. Broil the fish for 3–4 minutes, or until the salmon is cooked and the lime has caramelized. Sprinkle with the poppy seeds and serve with steamed rice.

aromatic noodles
with seared salmon   serves 4

7 ounces soba noodles
2 tablespoons olive oil
four 6-ounce salmon fillets
1 teaspoon sesame oil
1 tablespoon finely grated fresh ginger
2 garlic cloves, crushed
2 large red chilies, seeded and finely
   chopped
4 scallions, finely sliced
1 teaspoon lime juice
1 tablespoon soy sauce
1 teaspoon fish sauce
1 bunch garlic chives (about 1 ounce),
   snipped into 3/4-inch lengths

Bring a large pot of water to a boil and cook the noodles until they are al dente. Drain and rinse under cold running water and set aside.

Heat a large frying pan or wok over high heat and add half the olive oil. When the oil is hot, add the salmon, skin side down, and cook for 1 minute. Turn over and cook for an additional 2 minutes before removing from the pan.

Drain the oil from the pan and return it to the heat. Add the sesame oil and the rest of the olive oil. Add the ginger, garlic, chilies, scallions, lime juice, soy sauce, and fish sauce. Stir-fry for 1 minute. Add the noodles, tossing until they are nicely coated. Remove from the heat. Add the chives. Toss again. Divide the noodles between four bowls and top with the salmon.

steamed fish
with fresh ginger

serves 4

four 4 1/2-ounce perch or other firm
  whitefish fillets
3 scallions, finely sliced diagonally
1 1/2-inch piece fresh ginger, julienned
1/3 cup peanut oil
lemon wedges, to serve
steamed white rice, to serve

Bring a large pot of water to a boil, then put a steamer basket on top. Steam the fish for 5 minutes, or until it is cooked through. Meanwhile, put the scallions and ginger in a metal bowl. Heat the peanut oil in a frying pan until it begins to smoke. Carefully pour the hot oil over the ginger and scallions and allow the oil to absorb the flavors.

Put the fish on warm serving plates and spoon the ginger oil over it. Serve with lemon wedges and steamed white rice.

lemon and saffron risotto

serves 4

4 cups vegetable stock (see basics)
3¹/₂ tablespoons butter
1 onion, finely diced
15 saffron threads
1¹/₄ cups arborio (risotto) rice
1 bunch asparagus
2 tablespoons lemon juice
³/₄ cup grated Parmesan cheese
sea salt and freshly ground black
  pepper, to season

Heat the stock in a saucepan over high heat. When it is almost boiling, reduce the heat to a simmer. Melt the butter in a heavy-based saucepan over medium heat. Add the onion and saffron, and cook until the onion is soft and transparent.

Add the rice and stir until the grains are glossy and well coated in the buttery saffron. Add 1 cup of the hot stock and stir until it is absorbed. Continue to add the stock until it is all absorbed and the rice is tender.

Bring a saucepan of water to a boil and quickly blanch the asparagus until it is bright green. Drain and slice into small pieces. Add the lemon juice and Parmesan cheese to the risotto and season with sea salt and freshly ground black pepper. Spoon the risotto into warm bowls and top with the asparagus spears.

wild mushroom spaghetti

serves 4

1/2 cup dried porcini mushrooms
3 tablespoons olive oil
2 garlic cloves, chopped
1 onion, finely diced
2 meadow mushrooms, finely sliced
2 cups shiitake mushrooms, sliced
1/2 teaspoon thyme leaves
1/2 cup white wine
1 1/2 cups enoki mushrooms
salt and pepper, to season
14 ounces spaghetti
3/4 cup finely grated Parmesan cheese

Bring a large pot of water to a boil for the spaghetti. Soak the dried porcini mushrooms in 1 cup of boiling water for 15 minutes.

Heat the olive oil and fry the garlic and onion over medium heat until they are translucent. Drain the porcini mushrooms, straining and reserving the soaking liquid. Roughly slice the soaked mushrooms and add them to the onions. Add the meadow mushrooms, shiitake mushrooms, and thyme. Cook them until the meadow mushrooms are soft, then add the white wine, mushroom soaking liquid, and enoki mushrooms. Season and reduce the heat to a low simmer.

Cook the spaghetti until al dente, then drain and return it to the warm pot. Add the Parmesan cheese and stir through before dividing the pasta between four bowls. Top with the wild mushroom sauce.

seared snapper with lime salsa

serves 4

2 teaspoons fish sauce

2 tablespoons lime juice

4 tablespoons olive oil

1/2 teaspoon jaggery (or soft brown sugar)

1 ripe avocado, diced

1 lime, segments finely diced

1 short cucumber

1/2 red onion, finely diced

2 large red chilies, seeded and very finely sliced

1 handful cilantro leaves

sea salt and freshly ground black pepper, to season

four 7-ounce snapper or other firm whitefish fillets, skin on

Preheat the oven to 400°F. Put the fish sauce, lime juice, olive oil, and sugar in a bowl and stir until the sugar has dissolved. Add the diced avocado, lime, cucumber, onion, chilies, and cilantro leaves, and toss together. Season to taste with sea salt and freshly ground black pepper.

Rinse the fish fillets and pat them dry with paper towels. Put the vegetable oil in a large ovenproof frying pan over high heat. Season the fillets with sea salt and put them, skin side down, in the hot pan. Sear the fillets for a minute or two, or until the skin is crisp and golden, and then turn the fillets over.

Put the pan in the oven and bake for 8 minutes. Transfer to a serving dish and spoon over the salsa. Serve with boiled new potatoes.

pan-fried whiting with green bean, watercress, and fennel salad *serves 4*

1/4 cup lemon juice
1/2 cup olive oil
2 tablespoons finely chopped mint
2 tablespoons finely chopped dill
1 garlic clove, crushed
12 small whiting or other delicate
  whitefish fillets
2 handfuls picked watercress
3/4 cup green beans, blanched
1 fennel bulb, finely sliced

Put the lemon juice, olive oil, mint, dill, and garlic in a large bowl and mix well. Rinse the fish fillets in cold water and pat dry with paper towels. Toss the fillets in the marinade, cover, and leave in the refrigerator to marinate for a few hours.

Heat a large nonstick frying pan over high heat. Cook the whiting for 1–2 minutes on each side, then take the fillets out of the pan. Add any remaining marinade to the pan and cook for 1 minute.

Toss the watercress, beans, and fennel together and pile on four plates. Top with the fish and a light drizzle of the marinade sauce.

chinese omelets

serves 4

3 eggs
1 tablespoon mirin
1/2 teaspoon soy sauce
sea salt and freshly ground black
    pepper, to season
1 cup fresh crabmeat, shredded
1 teaspoon lemon juice
1 teaspoon olive oil
1 cup bean sprouts, trimmed
1/2 cup water-spinach tips
2 teaspoons vegetable oil
2 shallots, finely sliced on the diagonal
1 large red chili, finely sliced

Whisk together the eggs, mirin, and soy sauce. Season with a little sea salt and freshly ground black pepper and set aside. In a bowl, combine the crabmeat, lemon juice, and olive oil. Season with sea salt and pepper, and toss to combine. Add the bean sprouts and water-spinach tips, and set aside.

Heat a small nonstick frying pan over medium heat and add 1/2 teaspoon of the vegetable oil. Ladle in some of the egg mixture and gently swirl the pan around so that the egg finely coats the base of the pan. Continue to cook until the egg has cooked through, then remove by sliding the omelet onto a plate. Repeat with the remaining mixture, adding oil to the pan as it is needed, until you have four thin omelets.

Put each omelet on a serving plate, add the crabmeat mixture, and roll half the omelet over the filling. Sprinkle with the shallots and chili.

penne with arugula, chili, and parmesan cheese   serves 4

14 ounces penne pasta
1 chili, seeded and finely chopped
1 tablespoon salted capers
4 tablespoons extra-virgin olive oil
1 bunch arugula, rinsed and roughly
  chopped
1 cup grated Parmesan cheese

Bring a large pot of salted water to a boil and cook the pasta until al dente. Drain the pasta and then return it to the warm pot. Add the chili, capers, olive oil, arugula, and half the grated Parmesan cheese.

Toss the ingredients together until the arugula is slightly wilted, then spoon the pasta into four warm pasta plates. Sprinkle with the remaining Parmesan cheese and serve.

deep-fried whitebait serves 4

18 ounces whitebait
1 cup all-purpose flour
1/2 teaspoon paprika
1 teaspoon sea salt, plus extra to
  sprinkle
3 cups sunflower oil
lemon wedges, to serve
fresh bread, buttered, to serve

Rinse the whitebait under running cold water, then drain in a colander or large sieve. Put the flour, paprika, and sea salt in a large bowl and stir to mix well.

Heat the oil in a large, deep saucepan until the surface begins to shimmer and a pinch of flour dropped into the oil fries immediately.

Add the whitebait to the seasoned flour, tossing until all the fish are well coated. Using your fingers, lift the whitebait out of the bowl and shake it free of any excess flour. Deep-fry the whitebait in batches for 3 minutes, or until crisp and golden. Serve with a sprinkle of sea salt, lemon wedges, and slices of buttered fresh bread.

charbroiled bell pepper with boiled eggs and anchovies serves 4

4 red bell peppers
4 eggs, at room temperature
3 tablespoons extra-virgin olive oil
sea salt and freshly ground black
   pepper, to season
8 radicchio leaves
8 anchovy fillets
1 tablespoon salted capers

Charbroil or roast the red bell peppers until their skins are blackened. Place them in a bowl and cover with plastic wrap until they have cooled. Bring a pot of water to a boil and then add the eggs. Boil the eggs for 5 minutes, then remove them from the pot and allow to cool. Rub the blackened skin from the bell peppers, then cut or tear the flesh into long strips.

Put the strips in a bowl and add the olive oil and some sea salt and freshly ground black pepper. Toss to coat the bell pepper strips. Peel the eggs. Tear the radicchio leaves in half and divide them between four plates. Top with the marinated bell peppers, anchovies, and capers. Cut the eggs in half and add them to the salad. Drizzle with any of the remaining bell pepper oil and serve.

cod with lime-pickle sauce

2 large handfuls Italian parsley leaves
4 anchovies
1 teaspoon small capers
10 mint leaves
1 tablespoon Indian lime pickle
1/3 cup light olive oil
four 5 1/2-ounce cod or other firm
 whitefish fillets
2 tablespoons olive oil
boiled new potatoes, to serve

Put the parsley, anchovies, capers, mint, lime pickle, and light olive oil into a food processor or blender and blend to form a thick sauce. Set aside.

Rinse the fish fillets under cold running water, then pat dry with paper towels. Heat the oil in a nonstick frying pan over high heat and add the fish fillets. Cook for 2 minutes, then turn them over. Reduce the heat to medium and cook for an additional 3–4 minutes, depending on how thick the fillets are.

Serve the fish with a spoonful of the sauce and boiled new potatoes.

fresh egg-noodle salad

serves 4

7 ounces fresh egg noodles
1 cup finely sliced Chinese cabbage
2 scallions, finely sliced
1 cup bean sprouts
1 carrot, peeled and grated
1 red bell pepper, julienned
2 handfuls cilantro leaves
3 tablespoons hoisin sauce
1 1/2 tablespoons lime juice
1 teaspoon sesame oil
1 teaspoon sugar
2 tablespoons sesame seeds

Bring a large pot of salted water to a boil and add the egg noodles. Cook until al dente, then drain. Rinse under cold running water and set aside. Put the Chinese cabbage, scallions, bean sprouts, carrot, bell pepper, and cilantro in a large bowl.

In a small bowl, combine the hoisin sauce, lime juice, sesame oil, and sugar. Stir to combine, then pour the sauce over the vegetables. Rinse the noodles one more time under cold water, then drain and roughly cut the noodles with a pair of kitchen scissors. Add to the vegetables. Toss several times so that the noodles and vegetables are well coated in the dressing. Put the noodles in a large serving bowl. Toast the sesame seeds in a pan over medium heat until golden brown, then sprinkle them over the salad.

citrus compote breakfast trifles honey-toasted fruit
granola coconut bread banana pancakes with pineapple
syrup banana bread pineapple muffins quick fix baked
passion-fruit soufflés vanilla-poached apricots
nectarine and almond cake lemon ricotta cake
nectarine and hazelnut torte passion-fruit melting
moments white-peach ice cream almond and pine-nut
cake vanilla panna cotta with taffy apples vanilla-

04   sweets

poached white peaches with mint passion-fruit
custard with pistachio biscotti oatmeal cookies
chestnut cakes with lemon frosting marinated plums
with toasted pound cake citrus syrup cake creamed
rice with vanilla-glazed oranges pineapple fruit

citrus compote

makes 8-10 small servings or 4 regular servings

3 limes
3 oranges
2 pink grapefruits
1 vanilla bean, finely chopped
1 teaspoon sugar
1 cup yogurt
honey, to taste

Zest 1 lime and 1 orange, and put the zest in a bowl. Peel the limes, oranges, and grapefruits with a sharp knife. Cut the flesh into segments, or thinly slice, saving any juice. Add the vanilla bean, sugar, and reserved juice, and mix to combine. Serve with the yogurt and a drizzle of honey.

breakfast trifles

makes 8 small glasses

1¹/₂ cups yogurt
honey, to taste
2 cups toasted granola
2¹/₂ cups fruit of your choice, such
   as diced mangoes or peaches, or
   mixed berries

Stir the yogurt with honey, to taste, until it is smooth, creamy and well-combined. Layer the toasted granola, yogurt, and fruit into small glasses or bowls, finishing with fruit on top. Serve with a small spoon.

honey-toasted fruit granola

serves 12

5 cups rolled oats
1 cup unsalted sunflower seeds
1 cup slivered almonds
1 cup triticale
1 cup shredded coconut
2 tablespoons sesame seeds
3/4 cup honey
4 tablespoons vegetable oil
1/4 cup dried apricots, finely sliced
1/3 cup dried apples, finely sliced
2/3 cup dried peaches, finely sliced

Preheat the oven to 300°F. Put the oats in a large bowl. Add the sunflower seeds, slivered almonds, triticale, shredded coconut, and sesame seeds. Stir to combine.

Heat the honey and the vegetable oil in a saucepan over low heat. Pour the warm honey mixture over the dry ingredients and stir until they are well coated. Spread the mixture on a baking sheet and bake for 30 minutes, stirring occasionally. Remove from the oven and allow to cool. Add the dried apricots, apples, and peaches. Toss to combine. Store the granola in an airtight container.

coconut bread

2 eggs
1 1/4 cups milk
5 tablespoons unsalted butter
2 1/2 cups all-purpose flour
2 teaspoons baking powder
2 teaspoons ground cinnamon
1 cup superfine sugar
2 1/2 cups shredded coconut
banana, sliced, to serve

Preheat the oven to 350°F. Put the eggs and milk in a bowl and lightly whisk. Melt the butter and set aside. Sift the flour, baking powder, and cinnamon into a mixing bowl. Add the sugar and coconut. Make a well in the center and gradually stir in the milk mixture until fully combined. Add the melted butter and stir until the mixture is just smooth.

Pour the mixture into a greased and lined 4 x 8 1/4-inch loaf pan and bake for 1 hour, or until a skewer inserted into the center comes out clean. Allow to cool before removing from the pan. Serve in buttery toasted slices with or without sliced banana.

banana pancakes with pineapple syrup

pancake mixture
1 cup self-rising flour
1/4 cup superfine sugar
1/2 teaspoon salt
1 egg
scant **2/3 cup milk**

1/2 cup grated jaggery (or soft brown sugar)
1 cup fresh pineapple juice
1 tablespoon lime juice
2 bananas
2 tablespoons superfine sugar
2 tablespoons unsalted butter

To make the pancakes, put the flour, sugar, and salt in a bowl. In a separate bowl, beat the egg and milk together. Pour into the flour mixture and lightly fold together. Allow the batter to rest for 10 minutes before using.

To make the syrup, put the sugar and pineapple juice in a small saucepan over high heat and bring to a boil. Reduce the heat and simmer until the juice has reduced by half and formed a syrup. Remove from the heat and stir in the lime juice.

Slice the bananas thinly and toss the slices in the sugar. Heat a little butter in a frying pan over medium heat. Add a tablespoon of the pancake mixture to the pan and cook for 1 minute. Top with banana slices, and cook until bubbles appear. Flip the pancake over and cook for an additional 2 minutes. Remove and keep in a warm place. Repeat with the remaining batter and banana, adding more butter to the pan as required. Serve with a drizzle of the pineapple syrup.

banana bread

6¹/₂ tablespoons butter, softened
1/2 cup superfine sugar
2 eggs
1 teaspoon natural vanilla extract
2 cups all-purpose flour
2 teaspoons baking powder
2 large ripe bananas
1 orange, zested
honey or maple syrup, to serve

Preheat the oven to 350°F. Put the butter, sugar, eggs, vanilla extract, flour, baking powder, bananas, and orange zest in a food processor. Process to a smooth batter. Spoon into a greased and lined $3^1/4$ x $6^1/4$-inch loaf pan. Bake for 1 hour, or until a skewer inserted into the center comes out clean. Serve in warm slices or toasted with butter and a drizzle of honey or maple syrup.

pineapple muffins

makes 18

1³/4 cups all-purpose flour
2 teaspoons baking powder
pinch salt
³/4 cup sugar
1/2 teaspoon ground cinnamon
1¹/4 cups dried coconut
3 tablespoons unsalted butter, melted
³/4 cup milk
2 eggs
1 cup diced fresh pineapple

Preheat the oven to 350°F. Sift the flour, baking powder, and salt into a large mixing bowl. Add the sugar, cinnamon, and coconut, and stir to combine. Make a well in the center of the mixture and add the melted butter, milk, and eggs. Mix until just combined, then fold the pineapple through the batter.

Grease two mini muffin pans (lined with paper muffin cups, if desired) and put a heaping tablespoon of the mixture into each hole. Bake for 15–17 minutes, or until golden brown.

quick fix

4 puff pastry sheets
confectioners' sugar, to sprinkle
fresh berries, to serve
whipped cream flavored with natural
  vanilla extract, to serve

Preheat the oven to 350°F. Cut the puff pastry sheets into 1 1/4 x 3-inch strips. Put them on a greased baking sheet lined with parchment paper, and bake for 15 minutes, or until golden brown and crisp. Remove from the oven, sprinkle with sugar, and serve with berries and the vanilla-flavored whipped cream.

baked passion-fruit souffés

serves 6

½ cup sugar, plus extra for sprinkling
7 eggs, separated
4 tablespoons passion-fruit pulp
1 teaspoon cornstarch
confectioners' sugar, to serve

Preheat the oven to 400°F. Grease six 1¼-cup ramekins. Sprinkle the ramekin bases with sugar to coat, then tip out any excess sugar. Put 5 egg yolks (discard 2 yolks) into a metal bowl with the ½ cup sugar and whisk until very thick and pale yellow.

Put the bowl over a saucepan of simmering water and stir gently until the mixture thickens and is hot to touch. Remove from the heat and put the bowl into a sink filled with iced water. Stir until cool. Fold in the passion-fruit pulp. In a separate bowl, beat the egg whites until soft peaks form. Add the cornstarch and beat for 1 minute more. Fold half the beaten egg whites through the passion-fruit mixture until well blended, then lightly fold in the remaining egg whites.

Spoon the batter into the ramekins, filling to within about ½ inch of the top. Bake for 5 minutes, then reduce the temperature to 350°F and bake for an additional 12 minutes, or until the soufflés have risen and the tops are golden brown. Remove from the oven and sprinkle with confectioners' sugar to serve.

vanilla-poached apricots

serves 6

1 cup dried apricots
1 vanilla bean, halved lengthwise
1/2 teaspoon rosewater
1 tablespoon honey
1/3 cup toasted silvered almonds
1 cup plain yogurt or warm custard

Put the apricots in a saucepan with the split vanilla bean and 21/2 cups of water. Bring to a boil, then cover and allow the fruit to simmer on low heat for 1 hour.

Remove the vanilla bean and stir in the rosewater and honey. Serve with the toasted almonds and yogurt or a swirl of warm custard.

nectarine and almond cake

3 eggs
1/2 cup milk
11/3 cups superfine sugar
2 cups all-purpose flour
2 teaspoons baking powder
1 teaspoon natural vanilla extract
8 nectarines, pits removed
1/2 cup ground almonds
3 tablespoons unsalted butter

Preheat the oven to 350°F. Grease and line a 9-inch springform cake pan. Combine the eggs, milk, sugar, flour, baking powder, and vanilla extract in a food processor and process to form a thick batter. Scrape the batter into a bowl. Slice the nectarines into eighths and fold the fruit through the batter.

Spoon the batter into the prepared pan and top with the ground almonds and small pats of the butter. Bake for 40 minutes. Test with a skewer to ensure that the cake is cooked, then remove the pan from the oven and allow the cake to cool before serving.

lemon ricotta cake   serves 10

1 cup golden raisins
1 cup very strong Earl Grey tea
6 eggs, separated
2 cups firm ricotta cheese
1/2 cup heavy cream
1/2 cup superfine sugar
3 lemons, zested
lemon and Cointreau syrup (see basics)
vanilla ice cream (see page 282),
  to serve

Preheat the oven to 350°F. Line a 8-inch springform cake pan with parchment paper.

Put the golden raisins into the Earl Grey tea to soak. Whip the egg whites until stiff peaks form. Put the ricotta cheese, egg yolks, cream, sugar, and lemon zest in a large bowl and stir until combined. Drain the raisins and add them to the ricotta mixture before carefully folding in the beaten egg whites.

Pour the mixture into the cake pan and bake for 40 minutes. Put a layer of foil over the cake to keep it from burning, and bake for an additional 15 minutes. Test that the cake is firm—a skewer should come out clean when inserted into the center of the cake. Allow to cool in the pan before turning out. Serve with lemon and Cointreau syrup and vanilla ice cream.

nectarine and hazelnut torte

1/2 cup superfine sugar
1 cinnamon stick
1 vanilla bean, halved lengthwise
9 nectarines, pitted and quartered
4 eggs
2/3 cup confectioners' sugar
1/2 cup all-purpose flour
3 tablespoons ground hazelnuts
2 tablespoons butter, melted
whipped cream, to serve

Preheat the oven to 350°F. Put the sugar, cinnamon, and vanilla bean in a small saucepan and add 1 cup of water. Bring to a boil, then reduce the heat and simmer for 5 minutes. Add the nectarines and cook for 3 minutes. Remove with a slotted spoon and set aside in a bowl. Reduce the syrup by half, then pour it over the nectarines. Allow to cool.

Put the eggs and confectioners' sugar in a heatproof bowl and set over a saucepan of boiling water, making sure the base of the bowl does not touch the water. Beat until the mixture is just warm, then remove from the heat. Continue to beat until it triples in volume. Fold in the flour, ground hazelnuts, and butter. Spoon into a lined, shallow 9 1/2 x 13 1/2-inch cake pan. Bake for 20 minutes. Turn out onto a flat surface and cut into large squares. To serve, spoon the cooked nectarines over the cake, top with the whipped cream, and drizzle with a little of the fruit syrup.

passion-fruit
melting moments

¹/₂ cup unsalted butter, chilled and
  cubed
¹/₄ cup confectioners' sugar, plus extra
  for dusting
³/₄ cup all-purpose flour
¹/₄ cup cornstarch
1 tablespoon passion-fruit pulp

lime butter
4¹/₂ tablespoons unsalted butter,
  softened
1 cup confectioners' sugar
1 teaspoon grated lime zest
2 teaspoons lime juice

Preheat the oven to 315°F. Put the butter, sugar, flour, and cornstarch in a food processor and process in short bursts until the mixture just comes together. Fold the passion-fruit pulp through the dough. Pipe the mixture in 1 teaspoon amounts onto a baking sheet lined with parchment paper. Bake for about 15 minutes, or until the cookies are a pale golden brown. Remove and cool on a wire rack.

To make the lime butter, put the butter, sugar, and lime zest in a mixing bowl and beat until the mixture is white. Fold the lime juice through.

Join two cookies together with lime butter and lightly dust with sugar. Repeat with the other cookies.

white-peach ice cream

serves 6

3 large white peaches, pitted and
  peeled
3 tablespoons Cointreau
2 tablespoons lemon juice
1 teaspoon rosewater
4–6 tablespoons superfine sugar
1 1/4 cups whipping cream, whipped
1/2 cup toasted almond flakes

Cut the peaches into small cubes and mix them with the Cointreau, lemon juice, rosewater, and sugar, stirring until the sugar dissolves.

Fold the fruit into the whipped cream, then stir in the almonds to combine. Pour the peach ice-cream mixture into a 3 1/4 x 8 1/2 x 2 3/4-inch loaf pan or mold and freeze it overnight.

Unmold the ice cream by dipping the pan into hot water before turning it out. Serve the ice cream in slices on chilled plates.

almond and pine-nut cake

serves 8

3 tablespoons unsalted butter
2 mandarins
1 2/3 cups raw almonds
1 1/3 cups superfine sugar
1/2 teaspoon ground cinnamon
8 egg whites
pinch salt
2/3 cup all-purpose flour, sifted
4 tablespoons pine nuts
3 tablespoons dessert wine or Grand
  Marnier
confectioners' sugar, to dust
mandarin salad (see basics), to serve
whipped cream, to serve

Preheat the oven to 350°F. Grease an 8-inch springform cake pan with the butter. Peel the mandarins and, with a sharp knife, finely chop the zest. Put 3 tablespoons of the zest in a food processor. Add the almonds, sugar, and ground cinnamon, and process to a fine consistency.

Beat the egg whites with the salt until stiff peaks form. Lightly fold the almond mixture into the egg whites, and then add the flour. Spoon the batter into the prepared pan and sprinkle with the pine nuts. Bake for 1 hour, or until a skewer inserted into the center of the cake comes out clean. Allow to cool before serving.

Pour the dessert wine or Grand Marnier over the cake, then dust with confectioners' sugar. Serve with the mandarin salad and whipped cream.

vanilla panna cotta with taffy apples

serves 8

3¹/2 cups whipping cream
2 lemons, juiced and zest finely grated
¹/2 cup superfine sugar
2 vanilla beans, halved lengthwise
3 gelatin sheets
taffy apples (see basics), to serve

Whip 1 cup of the cream and put it in the refrigerator. Put the remaining cream, lemon juice and zest, sugar, and vanilla beans in a saucepan and heat gently over low heat to melt the sugar. Do not let it boil.

Take the pan off the heat and, using the end of a sharp knife, scrape the seeds from the inside of each of the vanilla pods into the cream mixture (you can keep the pods for later use). Soak the gelatin sheets in a bowl of cold water. When the sheets are soft, squeeze out any excess water and stir them into the warm vanilla cream.

Allow the vanilla cream to cool before lightly folding through the reserved whipped cream. Pour the mixture into 8 teacups or molds, cover with plastic wrap, and chill in the refrigerator for 3 hours or overnight. The panna cottas can be served in their cups, or you can turn them out by dipping the base of each of the molds into a bowl of hot water and upending them onto the plate. Give them a little shake to loosen them. Serve with warm taffy apples.

vanilla-poached white peaches with mint

serves 6

2 cups sugar
2 vanilla beans, halved lengthwise
6 ripe white peaches, pitted and
  cut in half
1 tablespoon lemon juice
20 mint leaves, to garnish
vanilla ice cream (see page 282),
  to serve

Put the sugar and vanilla beans in a large saucepan with 4 cups of water. Bring to a boil and simmer for a few minutes. Add the peaches to the saucepan, skin side up, and cook for 2 minutes. With a large spoon, carefully turn the peaches over and cook for a few additional minutes. Depending on the size of the peaches, you may have to do this in batches. With the point of a sharp knife, test to see if the peaches are cooked. They should still be firm but give little resistance to the knife. Remove with a slotted spoon and put in a large bowl. Leave the syrup on the heat to reduce for a few minutes.

Carefully peel the peaches, then pour the syrup over them and set aside to cool. When the syrup has cooled, add the lemon juice and mint leaves. Serve with vanilla ice cream.

passion-fruit custard with
pistachio biscotti   serves 4-6

5 passion fruits
3 tablespoons unsalted butter
2 tablespoons superfine sugar
1 whole egg
1 egg yolk
2 teaspoons lime juice
1/3 cup whipping cream, whipped
pistachio biscotti (see basics), to serve

Remove the pulp from 3 of the passion fruits and strain through a fine sieve, stirring to push the passion-fruit juice through. Discard the strained pulp. Put the juice in a bowl with the unstrained pulp of the remaining passion fruits. Melt the butter in a small saucepan over low heat. When the butter has just melted, add the sugar, passion-fruit pulp, egg, and egg yolk. Whisk over medium heat until the mixture is thick and just boiling. Remove from the heat, stir through the lime juice, and refrigerate when cool. Fold the passion fruit through the whipped cream just before serving with pistachio biscotti.

oatmeal cookies

makes 30

1 cup all-purpose flour
1 cup rolled oats
1 cup dried coconut
1 cup sugar
pinch salt
1/2 cup unsalted butter
3 tablespoons dark corn syrup
1 teaspoon baking soda

Preheat the oven to 350°F. Grease and line a baking sheet with parchment paper. Sift the flour into a mixing bowl and add the rolled oats, coconut, sugar, and salt. Put the butter and corn syrup in a saucepan. Stir over low heat until the butter has melted. Put 2 tablespoons of boiling water in a cup and dissolve the baking soda. Stir the water and soda into the melted butter, which will cause it to bubble up, then pour it over the dry ingredients. Stir to combine.

Drop spoonfuls of the mixture onto the baking sheet, allowing room for the cookies to spread. Bake for 12–15 minutes, or until dark gold. Remove from the oven and transfer the cookies to a wire rack to cool. Store in an airtight container.

chestnut cakes
with lemon frosting

makes 12

6 eggs
2/3 cup superfine sugar
13/4 cups canned chestnut puree
13/4 cups ground almonds
1 teaspoon baking powder
1 quantity lemon frosting (see basics)

Preheat the oven to 350°F. Beat the eggs until light and fluffy, then add the sugar and chestnut puree, and beat for an additional 1 minute. Fold in the ground almonds and baking powder.

Spoon the mixture into a lightly greased 12-hole muffin pan (lined with paper muffin cups, if desired) and bake for 20 minutes, or until the cakes are cooked—a skewer should come out clean when inserted into the center of a cake. Remove the cakes and allow them to cool before covering with lemon frosting.

marinated plums with toasted pound cake serves 4

5 ripe plums, pitted and finely sliced
2 tablespoons superfine sugar
1/2 vanilla bean, finely chopped
1/2 cup dessert wine
4 slices ready-made pound cake
vanilla ice cream (see page 282),
  to serve

Put the sliced plums, sugar, vanilla bean, and dessert wine in a bowl. Stir, then cover with plastic wrap and chill in the refrigerator for several hours until you are ready to serve.

Take the plums out of the refrigerator. Broil the slices of pound cake on both sides until they are lightly browned. Put the slices of cake on dessert plates, top with the marinated plums, drizzle with any remaining juice, and serve with a scoop of vanilla ice cream.

citrus syrup cake   serves 10

1 cup unsalted butter, softened
1 cup superfine sugar
4 eggs, lightly beaten
2 cups self-rising flour, sifted
4 oranges
4 lemons
4 limes
1 cup sugar

Preheat the oven to 350°F. Grease and line a 9-inch springform cake pan. Beat the butter and superfine sugar in a mixing bowl until pale and creamy. Stir in the eggs, then fold in the flour. Spoon the batter into the cake pan and bake for 50 minutes, or until a skewer inserted into the center of the cake comes out clean.

Meanwhile, make the syrup. Juice and zest the oranges, lemons, and limes. Combine the juice with the sugar in a saucepan over medium heat and stir for about 20 minutes, or until the sugar dissolves and a clear syrup forms. Add the zest and simmer for 1 minute, then remove from the heat. Leave the cooked cake in the pan and pierce it all over with a skewer. Pour most of the syrup over the cake, reserving some of the syrup and all of the zest. When the cake has cooled, transfer it to a serving plate and spoon over the remaining syrup and the zest.

creamed rice with vanilla-glazed oranges

serves 6

1/2 cup short-grain rice
2 cups milk
1 vanilla pod, halved lengthwise
4 strips lemon zest
4 tablespoons sugar
1/2 cup whipping cream, whipped
vanilla-glazed oranges (see basics)

Preheat the oven to 350°F. Rinse the rice in cold water and drain it. Put the milk in a saucepan with the vanilla pod, lemon zest, and sugar. Bring to a boil, then add the rice and simmer gently for 30 minutes, stirring occasionally.

When the rice has cooked, allow it to cool a little and then fold in the whipped cream. Spoon the creamed rice into bowls and serve with the vanilla-glazed oranges.

pineapple fruit salad serves 4

1 pineapple
10 mint leaves
2 teaspoons finely grated fresh ginger
1 teaspoon orange-flower water
vanilla ice cream (see page 282) or
   yogurt and honey, to serve

Skin the pineapple, cutting out any brown "eyes." Cut it into thin slices lengthwise, trimming off any bits of woody core. Put the slices in a bowl along with the mint, ginger, and orange-flower water. Toss to combine, then cover and chill for 1 hour in the refrigerator. Serve with vanilla ice cream or yogurt drizzled with honey.

lemon delicious   serves 8

2 lemons
3 eggs
5 tablespoons unsalted butter
3/4 cup superfine sugar
3 tablespoons sifted all-purpose flour
3/4 cup milk
confectioners' sugar, to dust

Preheat the oven to 350°F. Grease a large ovenproof dish. Finely grate the zest of the lemons, then juice them. Separate the eggs.

In a bowl, beat the butter with the sugar and the grated lemon zest until pale and creamy. Add the egg yolks and whisk to combine. Whisk in the flour and milk, adding them alternately to make a smooth batter. Add the lemon juice and stir to ensure it is well combined. In a separate bowl, whisk the egg whites until they form stiff peaks and then lightly fold them into the batter. Pour the mixture into the prepared dish and put the dish in a large roasting pan. Fill the pan with enough hot water to reach halfway up the side of the dish. Bake for 1 hour. Dust lightly with confectioner's sugar before serving.

vanilla ice cream

1 1/2 cups milk
1 cup whipping cream
2 vanilla beans
5 egg yolks
heaping 1/2 cup superfine sugar

Put the milk and cream in a heavy-based saucepan. Lightly rub the vanilla beans between your fingers to soften them. Cut the pods in half lengthwise and put them in the pan. Put over medium heat and bring the milk and cream just to the simmering point. Remove from the heat.

Whisk the egg yolks with the sugar in a bowl until light and foamy. Whisk in a little of the warm milk and cream. Add the remaining liquid, reserving the vanilla beans, and whisk to combine. Return the mixture to the cleaned saucepan. Cook over medium heat, stirring constantly with a wooden spoon, until the mixture thickens and coats the back of the spoon. Strain into a bowl. Scrape the vanilla seeds from the split pods into the mixture and stir through.

Allow to cool before churning in an ice-cream machine according to the manufacturer's instructions.

lemon slices

1/2 cup unsalted butter, softened
1/2 cup confectioners' sugar, sifted,
   plus extra for dusting
1 teaspoon natural vanilla extract
scant 11/2 cups self-rising flour, sifted
1 teaspoon plus 2 tablespoons grated
   lemon zest
3/4 cup all-purpose flour
1/2 teaspoon baking powder
3/4 cup ground almonds
3 eggs
1 cup superfine sugar
3/4 cup lemon juice

Preheat the oven to 350°F. Grease and line a 61/4 x 101/2-inch pan. Beat the butter and confectioners' sugar in a mixing bowl until pale and creamy. Add the vanilla extract. Stir in the self-rising flour and 1 teaspoon of lemon zest. Press the mixture into the pan and bake for 15 minutes, or until golden.

Meanwhile, sift the all-purpose flour and baking powder into a bowl. Add the ground almonds. In a separate bowl, beat together the eggs, sugar, lemon juice, and 2 tablespoons lemon zest. Stir the egg mixture into the dry ingredients and pour over the already-cooked cake base. Bake for 20 minutes, or until firm. Cool in the pan. Cut into pieces and dust with confectioners' sugar.

mandarin cupcakes   makes 16

3 mandarins, peeled
6 eggs
2/3 cup superfine sugar
13/4 cups ground almonds
1 teaspoon baking powder
1/2 cup mandarin juice
1/4 cup superfine sugar, extra
poppy seeds, to sprinkle

Preheat the oven to 350°F. Put the mandarins in a large saucepan and cover them with water. Bring to a boil and then simmer for 2 hours. Drain the mandarins, allow them to cool, then break them into segments and pick out any seeds.

Put the fruit and skin in a blender or food processor and puree them. Beat the eggs until light and fluffy, then add the sugar and beat for 1 minute more before folding in the ground almonds, baking powder, and mandarin puree. Pour the mixture into two greased muffin pans (the holes lined with paper muffin cups if desired) and bake for about 20 minutes.

Put the mandarin juice and sugar in a saucepan, bring to a boil, and simmer for 5 minutes, or until the amount of liquid has reduced by half. Remove the cakes from the muffin pans, spoon over the mandarin syrup while they are still warm, and sprinkle with poppy seeds.

lemon sorbet

1 cup sugar
2 lemons, zest finely grated
5 lemons, juiced
1 egg white

Put the sugar and 1 cup of water in a saucepan over high heat. Stir until the sugar has dissolved, then remove the pan from the heat. Stir in the zest and juice. Allow to cool, then transfer to a container, cover, and refrigerate for 1 hour.

Churn the chilled liquid in an ice-cream machine according to the manufacturer's instructions. Whisk the egg white in a bowl until light and frothy. After 30 minutes of churning, add the egg white to the sorbet mixture in the ice-cream machine and continue to churn until the sorbet is firm. Serve immediately or store in a covered container in the freezer.

almond macaroons with passion fruit

makes 20

2 large eggs, separated (discard the yolks)
1 cup superfine sugar
2 1/4 cups ground almonds
1 teaspoon natural vanilla extract
confectioners' sugar, to dust
crème fraîche, to serve
fresh passion-fruit pulp, to serve

Preheat the oven to 350°F. Whisk the egg whites and sugar for 5 minutes, or until the mixture is light and fluffy, then fold in the ground almonds and vanilla. Drop large spoonfuls of the mixture onto baking sheets lined with parchment paper and bake for 15 minutes, or until the macaroons are pale brown. Allow to cool before removing them from the baking sheet.

Serve dusted with the confectioners' sugar and topped with crème fraîche and some fresh passion fruit.

bread and butter pudding

serves 6

1-pound loaf brioche
1 teaspoon ground cinnamon
3 eggs
3 tablespoons superfine sugar
2 cups whipping cream
4 tablespoons dark corn syrup
fresh berries, to serve

Preheat the oven to 350°F. Lightly butter a ceramic baking dish. Remove the crusts from the brioche, slice the brioche, then cut the slices into neat triangles. Arrange the triangles over the base of the baking dish and lightly sprinkle with the cinnamon. Put the eggs, sugar, and cream in a bowl and whisk together.

Pour the cream mixture over the brioche and drizzle the corn syrup over the top. Bake for 25 minutes, or until the pudding is set and golden brown. Serve with fresh berries.

tapioca pudding

makes 10 small servings

1/4 cup tapioca
1/4 cup superfine sugar
2 cups milk
1 sheet gelatin
1/3 cup toasted and finely chopped hazelnuts
1/4 teaspoon grated nutmeg
2 tablespoons bitter orange marmalade
2/3 cup whipping cream, whipped
fresh berries or poached fruit, to serve

Put the tapioca, sugar, and milk in a saucepan and bring to a boil. Reduce the heat and simmer for 20 minutes, or until the tapioca is soft and cooked. Set aside to cool slightly.

Soak the gelatin in cold water until soft, squeeze off any excess water, and add the gelatin to the warm tapioca mixture. Allow to cool completely. When the mixture has cooled, fold through the hazelnuts, nutmeg, and marmalade. Stir to combine the ingredients, then fold in the whipped cream. Spoon into ten small glasses and chill. To serve, top with fresh berries or poached fruit.

mango and orange hearts

1 mango
1/2 lemon, juiced
6 sheets gelatin
1/2 cup sugar
1 1/2 cups freshly squeezed orange juice
whipping cream, to serve
lime wedges, to serve

Puree the flesh of the mango with the lemon juice. Pour it into a liquid measuring cup, ensuring that there is 1 cup of liquid. If it is a little under, top it off with water or orange juice. Set aside.

Fill a large bowl with cold water and soak the gelatin sheets. Meanwhile, put the sugar and orange juice in a small saucepan. Heat, stirring, until the sugar has dissolved, then remove the pan from the heat and pour the syrup into a bowl. Squeeze the water from the gelatin before adding the gelatin to the syrup. Stir to dissolve and then add the reserved pureed mango. Ladle the liquid into six 1/2-cup heart-shaped ramekins or molds and put them in the refrigerator for a few hours.

To remove the jellies from the molds, dip the base of the molds in warm water and then turn the jellies out onto a plate. Serve with whipping cream and a squeeze of fresh lime juice.

shortbread

1 1/2 cups all-purpose flour
3/4 cup rice flour
pinch salt
3/4 cup plus 1 tablespoon unsalted
   butter, softened
1/3 cup superfine sugar, plus
   2 tablespoons for sprinkling
2 teaspoons finely chopped lemon zest

Preheat the oven to 375°F. Grease an 8 x 12-inch baking tray and line it with parchment paper. Sift the flours and salt into a bowl.

Cream the butter and 1/3 cup sugar until light and fluffy, then fold through the sifted flour until just combined. Press the mixture into the prepared baking tray and prick all over with a fork. Use a sharp knife to mark 1 1/4-inch squares. Bake for 5 minutes, then reduce the oven temperature to 315°F and cook for an additional 15–20 minutes, or until the shortbread is a pale golden color.

Sprinkle the zest over the top of the shortbread and cook for an additional 5 minutes. Remove from the oven and sprinkle with the 2 tablespoons of sugar while still warm. Cut into squares and cool on a wire rack.

lemon and coconut tart

serves 8

1/2 cup unsalted butter
11/2 cups superfine sugar
4 large eggs
11/4 cups plain yogurt
1 teaspoon natural vanilla extract
3 tablespoons lemon juice
2 tablespoons lemon zest
1 cup dried coconut
1 prebaked 10-inch short-crust tart
  shell (see basics)
confectioners' sugar, to dust
whipping cream or vanilla ice cream
  (see page 282), to serve

Preheat the oven to 350°F. Beat the butter and sugar together until they are light and creamy. Add the eggs one at a time and beat them into the mixture before adding the yogurt, vanilla, lemon juice, and lemon zest. Add the coconut and pour the mixture into the prebaked tart shell.

Bake for 30 minutes, or until the filling is golden and puffed. Dust with sugar and serve warm with cream or vanilla ice cream.

schnapps jellies   makes 24 squares

1 cup sugar
1 cinnamon stick
2 star anise
4 strips lemon zest
2 cups apple schnapps
12 sheets gelatin
3 sheets edible silver leaf

Put 2 cups of water in a saucepan with the sugar, cinnamon, star anise, and lemon zest. Bring to a boil, stirring to dissolve the sugar. Reduce the heat and simmer for 10 minutes. Cool slightly, then strain the syrup into a bowl and add the schnapps.

Put the gelatin sheets in a bowl of cold water and leave them to soften for 5 minutes. Squeeze the gelatin of any excess water and add it to the warm schnapps. Stir until the gelatin has dissolved, then pour the liquid into an 8 x 12-inch baking tray lined with plastic wrap. Lay the sheets of silver leaf over the surface of the jelly. Chill for several hours or overnight, then cut into squares to serve.

orange poppy-seed cake

serves 10

1 cup unsalted butter, softened
1 cup superfine sugar
3 eggs, lightly beaten
2 tablespoons poppy seeds
1 tablespoon grated orange zest
1/2 cup milk
2 cups self-rising flour, sifted
orange frosting (see basics)

Preheat the oven to 350°F. Grease and line a 9-inch springform cake pan. Beat the butter and sugar in a large mixing bowl. Add the eggs, poppy seeds, orange zest, and milk. Stir to combine and then fold in the flour. Spoon the batter into the prepared cake pan and bake for 1 hour, or until a skewer inserted into the center of the cake comes out clean. Turn out onto a wire rack to cool. When the cake has cooled, transfer it to a plate and spread with orange frosting.

ice cream with wafers   makes 5

1/3 cup dried coconut
1/4 cup superfine sugar
1 teaspoon all-purpose flour
1/4 teaspoon baking powder
3 tablespoons unsalted butter, melted
1 egg white
2 cups vanilla ice cream (see page 282), to serve

Preheat the oven to 315°F. Combine the coconut, sugar, flour, and baking powder in a bowl. Stir in the melted butter, then add the egg white and whisk until smooth.

Line a baking sheet with parchment paper and spread a tablespoon of the batter thinly over the parchment paper. Bake for about 7 minutes, or until the wafer is pale gold. Cool slightly, then cut into squares. Repeat until all the wafers have been cooked. Sandwich a slice of ice cream between two wafers and serve immediately.

sticky pineapple cake serves 8

1¹/₂ cups superfine sugar
2 cups dried coconut, lightly toasted
1 cup coconut milk
1³/₄ cups diced fresh pineapple
4 eggs
2 cups all-purpose flour
2 teaspoons baking powder

lime frosting
1¹/₂ tablespoons unsalted butter,
  softened
1 cup confectioners' sugar, sifted
2 tablespoons fresh lime juice

Preheat the oven to 350°F. Grease and line a 9-inch springform cake pan. Put the sugar, coconut, coconut milk, pineapple, and eggs in a large bowl and stir them together. Sift in the flour and baking powder and fold the ingredients together. Spoon the batter into the cake pan and bake for 1 hour.

To make the lime frosting, put the butter and sugar in a bowl and beat until the butter is worked into the sugar. Slowly add the lime juice so that the frosting is smooth and runny enough to be drizzled.

Test the cake with a skewer to see if it is cooked. Remove the cake from the pan, cool, and then gently drizzle the lime frosting over the cake.

papaya with
lemongrass syrup

serves 4

1 cup sugar
2 lemongrass stems, white part only,
   trimmed and bruised
1/2 cup passion-fruit pulp
2 small red papayas, sliced
vanilla ice cream (see page 282),
   to serve

Put the sugar and lemongrass in a saucepan with 1 cup of water, bring to a boil, then reduce the heat and allow the mixture to simmer for 10 minutes, or until it has reduced by half.

Add the passion-fruit pulp and stir it in before taking the pan off the heat and allowing it to cool. This syrup will keep for several days in a sealed jar in the refrigerator. For added flavor, keep the lemongrass in the syrup until you are ready to use it. Gently pour the syrup over the sliced papaya and serve with vanilla ice cream.

eccles cakes

1/3 cup dried peaches, chopped

1/4 cup currants

1/4 teaspoon ground nutmeg

1/4 teaspoon ground allspice

1/4 teaspoon ground cinnamon

1 teaspoon superfine sugar

2 tablespoons orange juice

1 teaspoon finely chopped orange zest

2 teaspoons finely chopped lemon zest

2 sheets ready-made puff pastry, thawed

milk, to glaze

confectioners' sugar, to dust

Preheat the oven to 350ºF. Put all the ingredients except the pastry, milk, and confectioners' sugar in a bowl and mix well. Stamp out ten rounds of pastry using a 3-inch cookie cutter. Put 1 teaspoon of the fruit mixture on one side of each pastry round and fold over to form a half-moon. Press the edges together with a fork or your fingers. With a sharp knife, make slits in the top of each pastry.

Put each pastry on a baking sheet lined with parchment paper and brush the tops with milk to glaze. Bake for 12–15 minutes, or until golden brown. Allow to cool and lightly dust with the confectioners' sugar.

apple vanilla ice with grapefruit

serves 4

4 tablespoons sugar
1 vanilla bean, halved lengthwise
1 green apple, grated
3/4 cup cloudy apple juice
2 ruby-red grapefruits, segmented,
  to serve

Put 2/3 cup of water, the sugar, and the vanilla bean in a saucepan and bring to a boil. Stir until the sugar has dissolved, then reduce the heat and stir in the grated apple. Remove from the heat and allow to cool.

Add the apple juice, stir, and tip the mixture into a plastic container. Put the container in the freezer for 1 hour. Remove and stir the mixture with a fork to break up the ice crystals. Return to the freezer for an additional 1–2 hours. Before serving, stir again with a fork. Serve with the grapefruit segments.

poached pears

serves 4

1¹/2 cups superfine sugar
1 vanilla bean, halved lengthwise
2 strips of lemon zest
4 pears

Put the sugar in a heavy-based saucepan with 4 cups of water, the vanilla bean, and the lemon zest. Bring to a boil over high heat, stirring until the sugar has dissolved. Remove from the heat.

Peel the pears, leaving the stems on. With the point of a small, sharp knife, remove the core from the base of each pear in one circular movement.

Cut a piece of parchment paper slightly larger than the size of the saucepan and crumple it. Stand the pears upright in the syrup and cover with the paper. Feel for where the stems are and cut the paper with small scissors so that the stems can stick through. Press the paper down.

Cover the saucepan with a lid, put over low heat, and gently simmer for 1¹/2 hours. Remove the saucepan from the heat and allow the pears to cool in the syrup.

caramel slices

1 cup all-purpose flour
6¹/₂ tablespoons unsalted butter
3 tablespoons superfine sugar

caramel
1¹/₄ cups condensed milk
2 tablespoons unsalted butter
2 tablespoons dark corn syrup

chocolate
1 cup chopped dark eating chocolate

Preheat the oven to 350°F. Grease and line a 6¹/₄ x 10¹/₂-inch shallow pan. Put the flour, butter, and sugar in a food processor and process until it comes together. Remove and press the dough into the base of the pan. Prick the dough with a fork and bake for 15–18 minutes, or until lightly golden.

To make the caramel, put the condensed milk, butter, and dark corn syrup in a saucepan over low heat and stir for 10 minutes. Do not boil. Remove from the heat and set aside to cool for 10 minutes. Pour the caramel over the baked cookie base and return to the oven for 10 minutes, or until the edges of the caramel begin to brown. Remove from the oven and allow to cool and set in the pan.

Melt the chocolate in a bowl set over a saucepan of simmering water, then spread it over the cooled caramel. Cut into pieces.

pear and jasmine tea sorbet

serves 4

1/4 cup lemon juice
4 Asian pears
1 1/2 cups jasmine tea
1/3 cup superfine sugar
fresh lychees, peeled, to serve

Put the lemon juice in a bowl. Peel, core, and chop the pears, adding them to the lemon juice as you go. This will prevent them from discoloring. Put the pears and 2 tablespoons of the lemon juice in a saucepan with the tea and sugar, and warm over medium heat. Simmer for 15 minutes, or until the pears have become opaque and soft. Blend to a fine puree, then pour through a fine sieve into a container. Allow to cool, then cover and put in the freezer for 3 hours or overnight.

Remove from the freezer and scoop into a food processor. Process, then freeze again. Serve scooped into bowls with fresh lychees on the side.

summer punch almond sherbet pear and honey smoothie cantaloupe and ginger whip egg flip tamarind and peach cooler lemon cheesecake drink pimm's classic summer morning mango, strawberry, and apricot chiller citron pressé piña colada fruit daiquiri lychee and champagne chillers banana cardamom lassi banana and honey smoothie mango lassi gin fizz kiwi and citrus cooler summer punch almond sherbet pear and honey

05 drinks

smoothie cantaloupe and ginger whip egg flip tamarind and peach cooler lemon cheesecake drink pimm's classic summer morning mango, strawberry, and apricot chiller citron pressé piña colada fruit daiquiri lychee and champagne chillers banana cardamom lassi

summer punch

ginger syrup

1/2 cup grated ginger
1 cup sugar

2 cups peach nectar
3/4 cup dark rum
1/4 cup lime juice
3 white peaches, peeled, pits
  removed, and finely sliced
1 cup chopped fresh pineapple
4 cups ginger beer or ginger wine
fresh lime and mint, to garnish

To make the ginger syrup, put the ginger, sugar, and 1/2 cup of water in a small saucepan and bring to a boil. Reduce the heat and simmer gently for 5 minutes. Strain into a container, cool, and store in the refrigerator until ready to use.

To make the punch, put 1/3 cup ginger syrup and the remaining ingredients (except the garnishes) into a punch bowl and stir well. Garnish with thinly sliced lime and torn mint leaves.

almond sherbet

serves 10

4 tablespoons ground almonds
1 cup sugar
4 split cardamom pods
1 teaspoon rosewater
2 drops natural almond extract
8 cups sparkling water
ice cubes, to serve

Put 3/4 cup of water and the ground almonds, sugar, and cardamom pods in a saucepan. Boil until the mixture thickens. Cool and add the rosewater and almond extract. Top off with cold sparkling water and ice cubes.

pear and honey smoothie

2 green-skinned pears, cores removed
1 tablespoon honey
1/2 cup plain yogurt
8 ice cubes

Put all the ingredients in a blender with 1/2 cup of water. Blend until smooth. Pour into glasses to serve.

cantaloupe and ginger whip

1 tablespoon chopped fresh ginger
2 cups chopped cantaloupe
1/2 cup orange juice
8 ice cubes

Put all the ingredients in a blender and blend until smooth. Pour into tall glasses to serve.

egg flip

serves 1

1 cup milk
1 tablespoon plain yogurt
1 egg
1 tablespoon honey

Put all the ingredients in a blender. Blend until the honey has dissolved, then pour into a chilled glass. Drink immediately.

tamarind and peach cooler

serves 2

2 tablespoons tamarind concentrate
2 ripe peaches, peeled, halved, and
    pitted
8 ice cubes
sugar, to taste

Stir the tamarind concentrate into 1 cup of water. Put the tamarind water, peaches, and ice cubes in a blender and blend until smooth. Taste and add a little sugar if desired. Pour into tall glasses.

lemon cheesecake drink

1/2 cup plain yogurt
1/4 cup whipping cream
2 tablespoons superfine sugar
2 tablespoons lemon juice
1/2 teaspoon natural vanilla extract
6 ice cubes
grated nutmeg, to serve

Blend the yogurt, cream, sugar, lemon juice, vanilla extract, and ice cubes in a blender. Pour into glasses and top with grated nutmeg.

pimm's classic

serves 1

2 fluid ounces Pimm's
2/3 cup dry ginger ale
1 teaspoon lime juice
ice
thin slices of orange, to garnish
cucumber strips, to garnish

Put the Pimm's, dry ginger ale, and lime juice in a chilled glass and top with ice. Stir to combine, then garnish with thin slices of orange and a few strips of cucumber.

summer morning

1/2 banana
1 cup chopped fresh pineapple
2 passion fruits, pulped
6 large mint leaves
8 ice cubes

Put all the ingredients in a blender. Blend to a smooth consistency and serve immediately in chilled glasses.

mango, strawberry, and apricot chiller

serves 2

1 mango
1 cup apricot nectar
6 strawberries
6 ice cubes

Peel the mango. Put the mango flesh and remaining ingredients in a blender and blend until smooth. Pour into tall glasses to serve.

citron pressé

sugar syrup
1 cup sugar

2 fluid ounces Absolut Citron vodka
2 tablespoons lemon juice
ice, to serve
lemon zest and peel, to garnish

To make the sugar syrup, put the sugar in a small saucepan with 1 cup of water and bring to a boil, stirring until the sugar dissolves. Cool, then store in a jar in the refrigerator until ready to use.

Put the vodka, lemon juice, and 1/4 cup of the sugar syrup in a small cocktail shaker. Shake and pour into a highball glass containing some ice. Garnish with lemon zest and a twist of peel.

piña colada

sugar syrup
1 cup sugar

1/2 cup chopped fresh pineapple
6 ice cubes
2 tablespoons lime juice
2 fluid ounces white rum
1/4 cup coconut milk
fresh pineapple and lime, to garnish

To make the sugar syrup, put the sugar in a small saucepan with 1 cup of water and bring to a boil, stirring until the sugar dissolves. Cool, then store in a jar in the refrigerator until ready to use.

Put 1/4 cup of sugar syrup and the remaining ingredients (except the fruit garnishes) in a blender and blend until smooth. Pour into cocktail glasses and decorate with pineapple wedges and thinly sliced lime.

fruit daiquiri   serves 2

2 tablespoons lime juice
2 teaspoons sugar
1/2 fluid ounce Triple Sec or Cointreau
4 fluid ounces white rum
1/2 cup diced mango
1/2 cup diced honeydew
6 ice cubes

Put all the ingredients in a blender. Blend and pour into two chilled glasses.

lychee and champagne chillers

serves 8

2¼ cups canned lychees
1 lime, juiced
champagne, to serve

Put the lychees and their syrup in a blender with the lime juice. Blend until smooth and then strain into a pitcher. Cover and put in the refrigerator for at least 1 hour to chill. Pour the lychee syrup into eight champagne or cocktail glasses and slowly top off each glass with champagne.

banana cardamom lassi serves 2

1 cardamom pod
1 banana, roughly chopped
1/2 cup plain yogurt
9 ice cubes

Remove the small seeds from the cardamom pod and put them in a blender along with the banana, yogurt, and ice cubes. Blend until smooth. Serve in chilled glasses.

banana and honey smoothie

1 banana, roughly chopped
3/4 cup plain yogurt
1 tablespoon honey
pinch of nutmeg
8 ice cubes

Put all the ingredients in a blender. Blend until smooth. Serve immediately.

mango lassi

3/4 cup roughly chopped mango flesh
1 teaspoon honey
1 teaspoon lime juice
1/2 cup plain yogurt
9 cups ice cubes

Put all the ingredients in a blender. Blend until smooth and pour into chilled glasses.

gin fizz

2 fluid ounces gin
1 tablespoon lemon juice
1 teaspoon superfine sugar
1 egg white
ice, to fill cocktail shaker
soda water, to serve

Put the gin, lemon juice, sugar, and a dash of egg white into a cocktail shaker filled with ice. Shake well and pour into a chilled tall glass. Top with soda water.

kiwi and citrus cooler

serves 4

sugar syrup
1 cup sugar

1 lime
1 lemon
1 orange
2 cups orange juice
4 kiwifruits, peeled
1/4 cup lime juice

To make the sugar syrup, put the sugar in a small saucepan with 1 cup of water and bring to a boil, stirring until the sugar dissolves. Cool, then store in a jar in the refrigerator until ready to use.

Segment the lime, lemon, and orange, and freeze in ice-cube molds filled with water. Combine the orange juice, kiwifruits, lime juice, and 2 tablespoons of the sugar syrup. Pour into glasses over the citrus cubes.

brioche dough harissa chicken stock lemon dipping sauce lemon mayonnaise dashi stock fish stock vegetable stock homemade pizza dough short-crust pastry lemon and cointreau syrup plum sauce lemon or orange frosting pistachio biscotti mandarin salad vanilla-glazed oranges taffy apples brioche dough harissa chicken stock lemon dipping sauce lemon mayonnaise dashi stock fish stock vegetable

06 basics

stock homemade pizza dough short-crust pastry lemon and cointreau syrup plum sauce lemon or orange frosting pistachio biscotti mandarin salad vanilla-glazed oranges taffy apples brioche dough harissa chicken stock lemon dipping sauce lemon mayonnaise

brioche dough

1/4 cup milk

2 teaspoons dry yeast

2 cups all-purpose flour

2 tablespoons superfine sugar

3 eggs

1 teaspoon sea salt

1/2 cup unsalted butter, softened

Heat the milk in a small saucepan until it is lukewarm. Remove from the heat and pour into the bowl of an electric mixer. Add the yeast and 3 tablespoons of the flour.

Leave covered for 10 minutes to activate the yeast. When the yeast mixture is bubbling on the surface, add the remaining flour, sugar, eggs, and sea salt, and begin to mix the dough on a low speed. After a few minutes, the dough should start to come together. Add the butter slowly and beat on a higher speed until the dough is shiny and elastic. Transfer to a bowl and cover with plastic wrap. Refrigerate for a minimum of 4 hours before use.

harissa

2 red bell peppers
3 red chilies
2 garlic cloves
1 tablespoon cumin seeds, roasted
  and ground
1 tablespoon coriander seeds, roasted
  and ground
1 large handful cilantro leaves
1 tablespoon pomegranate molasses
1 teaspoon sea salt
2¹/2 tablespoons olive oil

Preheat the oven to 415°F. Put the bell peppers on a baking sheet and bake for about 20 minutes, or until the skin is blistered and blackened. Remove and set aside to cool. When cool, remove the skin and seeds from the peppers and put the flesh in a food processor with the chilies, garlic, ground spices, cilantro, pomegranate molasses, and sea salt. Blend to a puree, then add the olive oil and process again.

chicken stock

makes 8 cups

1 whole fresh chicken
1 onion, sliced
2 celery sticks, sliced
1 leek, white part only, roughly
   chopped
1 bay leaf
2 Italian parsley sprigs
6 black peppercorns

Fill a large, heavy-based saucepan with 12 cups of cold water. Cut the chicken into several large pieces and put the pieces in the pan.

Bring the water to a boil, then reduce to a simmer. Skim any fat from the surface, then add the onion, celery, leek, bay leaf, parsley, and black peppercorns. Maintain the heat at a low simmer for 2 hours.

Strain the stock into a bowl and cool. Using a large spoon, remove any fat that has risen to the surface. For a more concentrated flavor, return the stock to a saucepan and simmer over low heat. If you are not using the stock immediately, cover and refrigerate or freeze. The stock will keep in the refrigerator for 2–3 days.

lemon dipping sauce

2 lemons, juiced
2 star anise
3 cardamom pods
1/4 cup sugar
2 teaspoons light soy sauce

Put all the ingredients in a small saucepan and simmer over medium heat for 5 minutes. Allow to cool before serving.

lemon mayonnaise

makes 1 cup

2 egg yolks
1 lemon, zested and juiced
1 cup light olive oil
sea salt, to taste

Whisk the egg yolks and lemon zest and juice together in a large bowl. While whisking, slowly drizzle in the olive oil until the mixture thickens, and keep whisking the mixture until it becomes thick and creamy. Season to taste with sea salt. If the mixture is very thick, add a little cold water until you achieve the right consistency.

dashi stock

makes about 8 cups

12 pieces dried kombu
1 tablespoon bonito flakes

Put the kombu and 8 cups of cold water in a large saucepan. Set over medium heat and slowly bring to a boil. Regulate the heat so that the water takes around 10 minutes to come to a boil. As it nears the boiling point, test the thickest part of the kombu. If it is soft to the touch and your thumbnail passes easily into the surface, remove it from the water.

Once the water is boiling, add 1/2 cup of cold water and the bonito flakes. When the stock returns to a boil, remove the pan from the heat and skim the surface of the stock to remove any muddy froth. When the bonito flakes sink to the bottom, strain the stock into a bowl through cheesecloth or a very fine sieve. The finished stock should be clear and free of bonito flakes.

fish stock

makes about 4 cups

2 1/4 pounds fish bones
1 onion, chopped
1 carrot, chopped
1 fennel bulb, sliced
2 celery sticks, sliced
2 thyme sprigs
2 parsley sprigs
4 black peppercorns

Put the fish bones in a saucepan with 8 cups of water. Bring to a boil, then reduce the heat and simmer for 20 minutes. Strain the liquid through a fine sieve into another saucepan to remove the bones. Add the onion, carrot, fennel, celery, thyme, parsley, and peppercorns. Bring back to a boil, then reduce the heat and simmer for an additional 35 minutes. Strain into a bowl and allow to cool.

vegetable stock

3 tablespoons unsalted butter
2 garlic cloves, crushed
2 onions, roughly chopped
4 leeks, white part only, roughly chopped
3 carrots, roughly chopped
3 celery sticks, thickly sliced
1 fennel bulb, roughly chopped
1 handful Italian parsley
2 thyme sprigs
2 black peppercorns

Put the butter, garlic, and onions in a large, heavy-based saucepan. Put the pan over medium heat and stir until the onion is soft and transparent. Add the leeks, carrots, celery, fennel, parsley, thyme, and peppercorns. Add 16 cups of water and bring to a boil. Reduce the heat and simmer gently for 2 hours. Allow to cool. Strain into another saucepan, using the back of a large spoon to press the liquid from the vegetables. Bring the stock to a boil, then reduce the heat to a rolling boil until the stock is reduced by half.

homemade pizza dough

makes 1 quantity pizza dough or 2 medium pizza bases, approximately 9 inches in diameter

2 teaspoons dried yeast or 1/2 ounce
    fresh yeast
1 teaspoon sugar
2 cups all-purpose flour
1 egg
2 1/2 tablespoons milk
1 teaspoon sea salt
olive oil

Put the yeast into a small bowl with the sugar and 1/4 cup of warm water. Stir lightly to combine. Set aside for 10–15 minutes, or until the mixture starts to froth. Sift the flour into a bowl and make a well in the center. Add the egg, milk, sea salt, and the yeast mixture. Gradually work the ingredients together to form a stiff dough.

Turn the dough out onto a floured work surface and knead until smooth and elastic. Oil a large bowl with a little olive oil and put the dough in it. Rub a little more oil over the dough before covering it with a damp cloth. Put the bowl in a warm place for 2 hours, or until the dough has doubled in size.

Preheat the oven to 400°F. Divide the dough in half and roll it out on a floured surface. Put each base onto a greased baking sheet and add your toppings. Bake for 15 minutes.

short-crust pastry

makes one 10-inch tart shell or 24 tartlet shells

1 2/3 cups all-purpose flour
7 tablespoons chilled unsalted butter,
  cut into cubes
1 pinch of salt for savory pastry, or
  1 tablespoon superfine sugar
  for sweet pastry

Put the flour and butter in a food processor. Add the salt or sugar and process for 1 minute. Add 2 tablespoons of chilled water and process until the mixture comes together. Wrap the dough in plastic wrap and chill for 30 minutes.

Using a rolling pin, roll out the pastry as thinly as possible over a floured surface, working from the center outward. Use the pastry to line a 10-inch tart pan or two 12-hole tartlet pans. Chill for an additional 30 minutes. Preheat the oven to 350°F. Prick the base of the pastry shell(s) with a fork, line with crumpled parchment paper, and fill with uncooked rice or baking weights.

Bake for 10–15 minutes, or until the pastry looks cooked and dry. Remove from the oven, remove the paper and rice or weights and allow to cool.

Uncooked tart shells that are not used immediately can be stored for several weeks in the freezer. To use, put the prepared tart shell into a preheated oven direct from the freezer to prevent the pastry from collapsing in on itself.

lemon and cointreau syrup

makes about $1/2$ cup

3 lemons, juiced
1/4 cup sugar
1 star anise
2 tablespoons Cointreau

Put the lemon juice, sugar, and star anise in a small saucepan. Bring to a boil, then reduce the heat, allowing the mixture to simmer for a few minutes. Remove from the heat and let it cool before adding the Cointreau. The syrup will keep for a couple of weeks in the refrigerator.

plum sauce

1 tablespoon Chinese black vinegar
1 tablespoon rice wine
2 tablespoons sugar
1 teaspoon light soy sauce
1 tablespoon vegetable oil
1 1/2 teaspoons finely chopped garlic
2 teaspoons grated fresh ginger
4 Satsuma plums, pitted

Put the vinegar in a small pitcher or bowl with the rice wine, sugar, soy sauce, and 1/2 cup of water.

Heat the vegetable oil in a small saucepan over medium heat and add the garlic and ginger. Fry for 1 minute, then add the plums. Cook until the plums are beginning to disintegrate, then add the vinegar mixture. Reduce the heat and simmer for 15 minutes, then remove from the heat and cool.

lemon or orange frosting

makes enough for a 9-inch round cake or 12 cupcakes

1 cup confectioners' sugar, sifted
**1 1/2 tablespoons unsalted butter,
  softened**
1 tablespoon lemon or orange juice

Blend the sugar, butter, and citrus juice in a mixing bowl. Depending on the desired thickness of your frosting, add a little more liquid, a few drops at a time.

Using a spatula or knife, spread the frosting over the cooled cake. To get a smooth surface, dip the spatula or knife in warm water before using it to smooth over the frosting.

pistachio biscotti

makes 30-40 cookies

1 cup all-purpose flour
1/2 cup superfine sugar
1 teaspoon baking powder
1 cup pistachio nuts
2 teaspoons grated orange zest
2 eggs, beaten

Preheat the oven to 350°F. Mix the flour, sugar, baking powder, pistachio nuts, and orange zest together in a large bowl. Make a well in the center and fold in the eggs to make a sticky dough. Turn out onto a clean floured work surface. Divide the dough into two sections and roll out each portion to form a log about 1 1/2 inches thick.

Put the logs onto a baking sheet lined with parchment paper, leaving space for each log to spread a little. Bake for 30 minutes. Remove from the oven and allow to cool.

Reduce the temperature to 275°F. With a sharp bread knife, cut each of the loaves into very thin slices, about 1/4 inch wide. Lay the cookies on a baking sheet and return them to the oven. Bake for 20 minutes, turning the cookies once. Remove from the oven and cool on wire racks.

mandarin salad

6 mandarins
1/2 teaspoon orange-flower water
**1/2 teaspoon finely chopped mandarin
zest**

Segment 4 of the mandarins and put the pieces in a bowl. Squeeze the juice from the remaining 2 mandarins and add to the segments. Add the orange-flower water and mandarin zest and stir together.

vanilla-glazed oranges

serves 4

1/4 cup superfine sugar
1/4 cup orange juice
1 vanilla bean, halved lengthwise
4 oranges, segmented

Put the sugar, juice, and vanilla bean in a saucepan and heat them gently together until the sugar dissolves. Turn up the heat and allow the mixture to bubble until it begins to turn thick, sticky, and taffylike.

Add the orange segments and stir them gently into the mixture so that they are completely coated in the taffy.

taffy apples

4 green apples, peeled, cored, and cut
  into eighths
3 tablespoons superfine sugar
1 teaspoon ground cinnamon

Toss the apple pieces with the sugar, cinnamon, and 2 tablespoons of water. Tip them into a heavy-based frying pan over medium heat and let them caramelize and brown. Turn each of the apple pieces as they begin to caramelize, and take them out when they are cooked on both sides.

glossary

Asian dried shrimp

Dried shrimp are available from most Asian grocery stores and can be bought either whole or shredded. They are used as a flavoring agent in many stocks, or as an ingredient in relishes and sambals.

balsamic vinegar

Balsamic vinegar is a dark, fragrant, sweetish aged vinegar made from grape juice. The production of authentic balsamic vinegar is carefully controlled. Bottles of the real thing have "Aceto Balsamico tradizionale de Modena" written on the label, while commercial varieties simply have "Aceto Balsamico de Modena."

basil

The most commonly used basil is the sweet Genoa variety, which is much favored in Italian cooking. Thai or holy basil is used in Thai and Southeast Asian dishes. To get the most out of fresh basil leaves, always tear them rather than chop them.

black sesame seeds

Mainly used in Asian cooking, black sesame seeds add color, crunch, and a distinct nuttiness to whatever dish they garnish. They can be found in most Asian grocery stores. Purchase the seeds regularly, as they can become rancid with age.

buttermilk

This low-fat dairy product is made from skim milk and milk powder, with a culture similar to yogurt. It is often used in baking (as a raising agent) and can be found in the refrigerator section of supermarkets. It has a tart taste.

cardamom

A dried seed pod native to India, cardamom is the third most expensive spice (after saffron and vanilla). The inner seeds when crushed give off a sweet, strong aroma. It is used whole or ground and can be found in the spice section of supermarkets. Cardamom should be used sparingly, as it has quite a strong flavor.

Chinese black vinegar

This rice vinegar is sharper than white rice varieties and is traditionally used in stir-fries, soups, and dipping sauces. The Chinese province of Chekiang has a reputation for producing the best black vinegars.

Chinese five-spice

An aromatic mix of ground spices, Chinese five-spice is made up of star anise, black pepper, fennel seeds, cassia, and cloves. It can be rubbed into the skin of chicken or duck or used sparingly to add an exotic flavor to pork or beef.

coconut cream/milk

Slightly thicker than coconut milk, coconut cream is available in cans. If you can't get hold of it, use the thick cream off the top of a couple of cans of coconut milk instead. Pour the milk into a pitcher and leave it to settle— the cream will separate out at the top.

cream

Cream comes with differing fat contents. If it needs to be whipped, it must have a fat content higher than 35 percent. Single and light cream cannot be whipped.

crème fraîche

A naturally sour cream that is lighter than sour cream. It is available at gourmet food stores and some supermarkets.

curry leaves

Small, green aromatic leaves of a tree native to India and Sri Lanka. They are usually fried and added to the dish or used as a garnish.

daikon

Daikon, or mooli, is a large white radish. Its flavor varies from mild to surprisingly spicy, depending on the season and variety. Daikon contains an enzyme that aids digestion. It can be freshly grated or slow-cooked in broths, and it is available from most supermarkets or Asian grocery stores. Select firm and shiny specimens with unscarred skins.

edible silver leaf

Silver leaf, or varak, is flavorless, safe to eat and available from Indian grocery stores. Both gold and silver leaf are also available from cake decorating shops. Both are extremely fragile. When using, remove the leaf from the paper it is attached to at the last minute by simply turning the paper over and applying the leaf to any surface or liquid.

enoki mushrooms

These pale, delicate mushrooms have a long thin stalk and tiny caps. They are very fragile and need only minimal cooking time.

fish sauce

This is a highly flavored, salty liquid made from fermented fish. It is widely used in south Asian cuisine to give a salty, savory flavor to dishes. Buy a small bottle and keep it in the refrigerator.

gelatin sheets

Gelatin sheets are available in varying sizes. Be careful to check the manufacturer's instructions reagrding which ratio of liquid to gelatin sheet to use.

Gruyère cheese

A firm cow's-milk cheese with a smooth texture and natural rind, Gruyère has a nutty flavor and melts easily, making it perfect for tarts and gratins. It can also be served as part of a cheese platter.

Hokkien noodles

Asian egg noodles used in soups and stir-fries. Hokkien noodles are precooked and just need to be heated—either softened in boiling water or fried. They are sold in Asian grocery stores and most supermarkets.

jaggery

Jaggery, or palm sugar, is obtained from the sap of various palm trees and is sold in hard cakes or cylinders and in plastic jars. If it is very hard, it will need to be grated. It can be found in Asian grocery stores and some supermarkets. Substitute dark brown sugar when jaggery is unavailable.

kaffir lime leaves

Also known as makrut leaves, the glossy leaves of this Southeast Asian tree impart a wonderful citrusy aroma. Always try to use fresh, rather than dried, leaves.

kecap manis

This is a thick, sweet-flavored soy sauce used in Indonesian cooking.

lemongrass

These long, fragrant stems are very popular in Thai cuisine. The tough outer layers should be stripped off first, and it can then be used either finely chopped or whole in soups. As its name suggests, it has a tart, lemony flavor. Lemongrass can be stored for up to 2 weeks.

mascarpone cheese

This heavy, Italian-style set cream is used as a base in many sweet and savory dishes. Very rich, it is perfect served with fresh fruit.

mirin

Mirin is a rice wine used in Japanese cooking. It adds sweetness to sauces and dressings, and it is used for marinating and glazing dishes like chicken teriyaki.

miso paste

An important ingredient in Japanese cooking, miso paste is made of fermented soybeans and other flavorings—wheat, rice, or barley. It is used as a flavoring and a condiment.

orange-flower water

This perfumed distillation of bitter-orange blossoms is mostly used as a flavoring in baked goods and drinks.

oyster mushrooms

These delicately flavored mushrooms are commonly a pale grayish brown or white but are also available in pink and yellow colors. Their flavor is sharp when raw, making them more suitable for use in stir-fried dishes.

pancetta

Pancetta is salted belly of pork. Pancetta is available either rolled and finely sliced or in large pieces ready to be diced or roughly cut. It adds a rich bacon flavor to dishes.

pickled ginger

Pickled ginger is available from most supermarkets. The thin slivers of young ginger root are pickled in sweet vinegar and turn a distinct salmon-pink color in the process.

pomegranate molasses

This is a thick syrup made from the reduction of pomegranate juice. It has a bittersweet flavor, which adds a sour bite to many eastern Mediterranean dishes. It is available from Middle Eastern grocery stores. The closest substitute is sweetened tamarind.

preserved lemon

These are whole lemons preserved in salt or brine for about 30 days, which turns their rind soft and pliable. Just the rind is used—the pulp should be scraped out and thrown away. Preserved lemon is an ingredient commonly found in Moroccan cooking. It is sold bottled and is available from supermarkets.

prosciutto

Prosciutto is lightly salted, air-dried ham. It is most commonly bought in paper-thin slices and is available from delicatessens and supermarkets. Parma ham and San Daniele are both types of prosciutto.

risotto rice

There are three well-known varieties of risotto rice that are widely available today: arborio, a large, plump grain that makes a sticky risotto; vialone nano, a shorter grain that gives a loose consistency but retains more of a bite in the middle; and camaroli, similar in size to vialone nano but which makes a risotto with a firm consistency. All are interchangeable, although cooking times may vary by about 5 minutes.

sambal oelek

A hot paste made from pounded chilies, salt, and vinegar, it is available from Asian grocery stores and most large supermarkets.

shiitake mushrooms

These Asian mushrooms have white gills and a brown cap. Meaty in texture, they keep their shape well when cooked. Dried shiitakes are often sold as dried Chinese mushrooms.

somen noodles

These thin, wheat-based Japanese noodles are commonly sold dried and in bundles. They are available from Asian grocery stores, and some supermarkets.

star anise

This is a pretty, star-shaped dried fruit that contains small, oval brown seeds. Star anise has a flavor similar to that of anise but is more licorice-like. It is commonly used whole because of its decorative shape.

sumac

Sumac is a peppery, sour spice made from dried and ground sumac berries. The fruit of a shrub found in the Northern Hemisphere, it is often used in Middle Eastern cuisine. Sumac is available from most supermarkets.

Szechuan pepper

This pepper is made from the dried red berries of the prickly ash tree, which is native to Szechuan in China. The flavor is spicy-hot and leaves a numbing aftertaste, which can linger for some time. Dry-fry and crush the berries for the best flavor. Japanese sancho pepper is a close relative of Szechuan pepper and may be used instead.

tamarind

Tamarind is the sour pulp of an Asian fruit. It is most commonly available compressed into cakes or refined as tamarind concentrate in jars. Tamarind concentrate is widely available; the pulp can be found in Asian grocery stores. To make tamarind water from compressed tamarind pulp, put 3 1/2 ounces of tamarind into a bowl and cover with 2 cups of boiling water. Allow to steep for 1 hour, stirring to break up the fibers, then strain. Use the concentrate according to package instructions.

tofu

Also known as soy bean curd, tofu is made from curdled soymilk, an iron-rich liquid extracted from ground, cooked soybeans. It is usually packaged in water and should be drained and covered in fresh water before storing in the refrigerator.

triticale

This grain is a cross between wheat and rye. It is highly nutritious and is often found in mixed breakfast cereals as well as soups and sweet dishes. It can be bought in health-food stores.

vanilla bean

This long, slim black bean has a wonderful caramel aroma that synthetic vanillas can never capture. Good-quality vanilla beans should be soft and not too dry. Store unused vanilla pods in a full jar of superfine sugar, which will not only help to keep the vanilla fresh, but the aroma of the bean will quickly infuse the sugar, making it ideal for use in desserts and baking.

water chestnuts

The edible tuber of a water plant, the water chestnut is white and crunchy and adds a delicate texture to many Southeast Asian dishes. Fresh water chestnuts can be bought at Asian grocery stores, but they are commonly available whole or sliced in cans.

water spinach

Also known as swamp spinach, water spinach has long, slender, graceful medium- to dark-green leaves. Although not related to common spinach, its flavor and fragrance resemble it. It is avialable in Asian markets and can be refrigerated in a plastic bag for up to 4 days.

index